W9-ASQ-656

FROM SEA TO
SHINING SEA

Also by Margaret Alison Johansen

HAWK OF HAWK CLAN

VOYAGERS WEST

In Collaboration with Alice Alison Lide

OOD-LE-UK THE WANDERER

PEARLS OF FORTUNE

DARK POSSESSION

THORD FIRETOOTH

SECRET OF THE CIRCLE

MYSTERY OF THE MAHTEB

THE WOODEN LOCKET

THE LAPLAND DRUM

MAGIC WORD FOR ELIN

917.3
J

FROM SEA TO SHINING SEA

How Americans Have Lived

by Margaret Alison Johansen

Illustrated by Bernard Case

IVES WASHBURN, INC.
New York

WINGATE COLLEGE LIBRARY
WINGATE, N. C.

COPYRIGHT © 1960 BY THOMAS EVAN LIDE, EXECUTOR OF THE
ESTATE OF MARGARET ALISON JOHANSEN

All rights reserved, including the right to repro-
duce this book, or parts thereof, in any form, except for the inclusion of brief quotations in a review.

Library of Congress Catalogue Card Number: 60-7107

MANUFACTURED IN THE UNITED STATES OF AMERICA

SURPLUS

DUPLICATE

COPYRIGHT OFFICE
AUG 30 1960
LIBRARY OF CONGRESS

In memory of my sister, Alice
Alison Lide, without whose effort,
research, and enthusiasm this book
would never have become a reality

19484

FOREWORD

From Sea to Shining Sea attempts to tell, in an informal way, the story of American family life from the coming of the first settlers to the present. Because of the richness of the source material, making the choice of what to use and what not to use has sometimes been painful.

Progress and building toward a better life are certainly part of our American tradition. From chapter to chapter I have tried to show this tradition in action. For instance, many of the items in the sections on education were chosen because they demonstrated progress from "book learning" for the favored few, to free compulsory schooling for every American child.

The medical material endeavors to carry forward several immensely important lines of medical progress as they touched family life. The agony of an amputation without anything to relieve the pain at last becomes modern painless surgery. Ignorance of the deadly bacteria lurking on hands, clothing, and in the air, finally yields to Lister's theory of antisepsis. Smallpox inoculation gives place to the vastly safer smallpox vaccination. Yellow fever and malaria, blamed upon the swamp miasmas, are finally traced to the mosquito. Because of lack of space, hundreds of equally wonderful medical miracles have had to be bypassed.

Home-building, in particular, shows the trend toward practical democracy. The stately Georgian mansions and handmade furniture of colonial days were for the enjoyment of the rich merchant and plantation owner. The invention of the circular saw and the brick-making machine, and the beginning of machine-made furniture, made it possible for families of modest means to build houses and furnish them comfortably.

The other subjects, each in its own way, move toward the ideal of more food, more books, more fun for everybody.

In every chapter I have purposely accentuated the typical, the popular. Mine is a recounting of the doings of an average family . . . and the average family was sometimes heroic, generally hard-working, frequently swept off its feet by enthusiasm for "what was new." But what fun folks had setting up housekeeping in Americanized Greek temples, furnishing Victorian Gothic villas with marble-topped black-walnut parlor suites, singing as they danced to "Waltz Me Around Again, Willie, Round and Round and Round." I admire them when they are brave, clever, industrious. But I love them when I see them going their rollicking way down the generations— meeting life with a smile. (And that is part of the American tradition, too.) It is my hope that boy and girl readers will also love them, and thus will be given a closer understanding of how their forefathers lived.

CONTENTS

Foreword   vii

Chapter 1. BOLD MEN IN SMALL SHIPS (1000–1564)   1

Chapter 2. SOLDIERS AND SETTLERS (1565–1606)   10

Chapter 3. THE HOME-BUILDERS (1607–1699)   29

Chapter 4. FRONTIERS OF FORTUNE (1700–1763)   49

Chapter 5. LET FREEDOM RING (1763–99)   69

Chapter 6. HAIL, COLUMBIA (1800–1824)   90

Chapter 7. HUSTLE AND BUSTLE (1825–49)   110

Chapter 8. FAMILY QUARREL (1850–74)   131

Chapter 9. HAPPY BIRTHDAY, U.S.A. (1875–99)   153

Chapter 10. TWENTIETH-CENTURY SPEED-UP (1900–
            1919)   174

Chapter 11. BOOMED, BUSTED, AND BETTERED (1920–
            39)   195

Chapter 12. A STANDS FOR ATOM (1940–60)   217

FROM SEA TO
SHINING SEA

Chapter 1

BOLD MEN IN SMALL SHIPS (1000-1564)

From that long-ago time when men first began to build and sail ships they held a dream in their hearts of a far, fair land beyond the ocean's blue rim. The Happy Isles or the Isles of the West was the name they gave to that land.

—Tradition

A TINY ship, its single square sail raised to the wind, beat its way westward over the gray Atlantic. Fifteen men were aboard—Leif Erikson and his crew and a Christian priest.

Seafaring was in Leif's blood. He was of that race of daring men known as the Northmen or the Norse, who for centuries past had sailed their dragon ships out of Norway's rockbound fjords. Leif's own father, a bearded giant of a man nicknamed Erik the Red, had dared the uncharted seas to discover and colonize a new land which he'd named Greenland.

Leif had been on a journey to Norway to spend a year at the king's court. Now he was returning to his home on Greenland.

The voyage that had begun under cloudless skies soon ran into heavy weather. Storm winds tossed and twisted the ship till it seemed as if the stout oak timbers must crack asunder. Then the winds stilled and a pall of thick white fog descended, blotting out sky and sea. Week after week the ship drifted helplessly, while men's eyes strove to pierce the chill white mists and find the sun or some star to guide by.

At long last the fog lifted. The lookout gave a loud cry. "Land! Land!"

All eyes turned toward the dark shape rising out of the sea to the westward. As the ship drew nearer the men saw hills covered with great trees. Of a certainty, these were not the ice mountains of Greenland.

Leif and his men went ashore. They marveled at all they saw for this was a land the like of which they'd never seen before. Here were golden sunshine, tall trees, and bright-hued flowers. Here were fish in the rivers and deer in the forest. But nowhere was there trace of human inhabitants.

"Let us stay here awhile and enjoy this land," said Leif. He caused trees to be cut down and they built a hut for shelter. They caught fish. They shot a wild deer with bow and arrow and made themselves a feast. Every day they went exploring along the sandy shore or back into the hills. They exclaimed over wide stretches of wild grain ripe for the harvest. These they called "fields of self-sown wheat." On the hill slopes they found vines bearing clusters of sweet wild grapes. Some of the grapes they crushed in a wooden trough and made into wine. Thereupon Leif said, "Let us name this beautiful land Wine Land, or Vinland. Aye, let it be called Vinland the Good."

Finally they boarded ship again and sailed on to Greenland. Leif promised himself that someday he would return to the fair land he had discovered, but he never did. In later times, however, the Norse skalds, the minstrels who made up songs about men who did heroic deeds, made up a song about Leif Erikson and the land he discovered—the land that is now known as the continent of North America. On wintry nights when men and women gathered round the hearth fire, the skald would strike his harp and sing:

> There was a man named Leif
> The son of Erik.
> In the year One Thousand
> After the birth of Christ
> Leif sailed from Norway.
> From Norway he sailed
> To carry the teachings
> Of the White Christ
> To far-off Greenland.
>
> Bravely the sea-horse
> Trod the gray waters.
> Loud howled the storm winds,
> High rolled the waves.
> Long was the ship tossed
> Upon the gray waters
> Till Leif land sighted,
> A land he knew not of.
>
> Skoal to Leif the son of Erik!
> Skoal to his wine-sweet land!
> Skoal to Vinland the Good!

Leif Erikson did not return to Vinland. But only a few years passed before a colonizing expedition set out from Greenland. This was under the leadership of the rich merchant, Thorfinn Karlsefni, and his wife, Gudrid the Fair. They had with them three ships and one hundred sixty men and women. They also brought cattle, sheep, and goats.

For a long time they sailed southward till they came to a

barren, stony land. They named this the Land of Flat Stones, and sailed on. They came to an island where some of the men went ashore and killed a bear. This place they named Bear Island. Again they sailed on. None of the shores they had come to answered the description Leif had given of his land.

Presently warm breezes began to blow from landward. The voyagers sniffed the scent of blossoms. Surely Vinland was not far off. Drawing close to shore, the three ships entered a bay protected by a curve of sandy beach. The rolling hills were dark with the green of trees and shrubs. Without doubt this must be the land Leif had told them of.

Down in the hold the bull was roaring and pawing as he sniffed the land scent. The sheep were giving vent to pitiful bleating. Up on deck the settlers crowded to the rail, all clamoring to set foot on that inviting shore. But Karlsefni held them back. Scouts armed with sword and spear and shield must first investigate whether wild beasts or wild men lurked in the forest depths.

It was a good report the scouts brought back. Here was a fair land. And nowhere was there trace of human inhabitants. No dwellings, no boathouses nor storehouses. This fine land was theirs for the taking.

So they went ashore, these tall blond Norsemen in bronze helmets and ring armor, and took the land for their own. They cut down trees and built strong timber houses. They tethered the cattle to graze on the lush green grass.

It was at this time that a son was born to Gudrid, the wife of Thorfinn Karlsefni, the head of the Vinland colony. They named him Snorri, and to him goes the honor of being the first white child born on the continent of North America.

The women took up their homemaking tasks. They milked the cows, and made the milk into butter and cheese. They ground the bread grain in small stone hand mills. The men felled more trees to get a shipload of timber to send back to Greenland. They explored deeper into the forest. But always they kept their eyes open for any glimpse of people native to this land.

Autumn passed into winter. One morning the watchman awoke the settlers with the shout, "They come! They come!"

Men in small skin canoes were paddling across the bay. They pulled their boats up on the sand, stared in wonder at the tall yellow-haired men and women facing them. The Norsemen stared back at them in contempt. Ha, these swarthy-faced black-haired strangers, naked save for an animal skin wrapped about their loins, were *Skraellings*—barbarians. For a while the two groups stood looking at each other, then the newcomers paddled away.

In the spring the Skraellings came again. This time they came to trade. They brought packs of furs for which the Norsemen traded strips of red cloth. But the bellowing of the bull frightened the forest men and they fled back to their boats.

Karlsefni's face was grim. "Mayhap they will come again," he said. "Not for trade, but for war." He gave orders for a strong palisade to be built around the timber houses. Men were bidden never to separate themselves from their weapons. Women and children must not stray from the palisade. A sentinel must stand guard every hour of the day and night.

Uneasy months dragged by. Then again came the watchman's warning shout.

The Skraellings came armed with arrows and slings, and they came in great numbers. The bay was darkened by their canoes. They made the air hideous with their yells.

The Norse struck deadly blows with swords and spears. But the Skraellings were too many; they pushed the Norsemen back. Then Karlsefni bethought him of the forest men's fear of the bull. He pricked the fierce animal with his sword and drove him, bellowing and brandishing his horns, straight at the enemy. With shrieks of terror the Skraellings fled.

The settlement was saved—but for how long? Without doubt the Skraellings would come again and again, and in ever greater numbers, till the Norse colonists were killed or driven out.

It now seemed clear to Karlsefni that though the land was good, their life here would be one of dread and constant struggle. The decision was cast to return to their own country. The child, Snorri, was three winters old when they left Vinland.

The Norse settlers were too few. The Skraellings were too many. Not yet was the Age of Gunpowder when one man with a gun could stand off a hundred men armed with bows and arrows; when a handful of bold adventurers could dominate a whole New World. Now and again some square-sailed ship crossed the wide North Atlantic, then the viking voyagers came no more. Mists of time closed over Vinland. But the story of a land once discovered lived on in men's memories.

Another age brought new adventurers. Nearly five hundred years after Leif Erikson first sighted the shores of Vinland the Good, another man of daring was readying his ships to try the Atlantic crossing.

On August 3, 1492, half an hour before sunrise, Christopher Columbus set sail from Palos, Spain, with three small ships and one hundred twenty men. Into the unknown sailed the *Santa Maria*, the *Pinta*, and the *Niña*, captained by Columbus who believed that the world was round, manned by sailors who feared that the world was flat and that sooner or later their ship would drop off the edge. The captain took bearings with a crude compass and by the stars. Cooking was done on deck upon a bricked hearth. By night a tarred rope, burning in a lantern, was hung from the stern. The largest of the ships had only a ninety-foot length and twenty-foot beam, but on they sailed, a thousand miles of ocean behind, uncharted thousands of miles before them.

On the twelfth of October, 1492, Christopher Columbus landed on an island in the West Indies, planted a cross, and claimed a New World for Their Majesties of Spain, the royal Ferdinand and Isabella.

Columbus had no trail to guide him across the wide expanse of the South Atlantic, but his three tiny vessels left trails that others quickly followed. Ships began to plow the ocean westward. Wallowing broad-beamed caravels spread three-cornered sail to the wind. Galleys came propelled by oars and sail. Splendid high-decked galleons, armed with cannon and a fearsome ironclad beak, came under full spread of canvas.

Amerigo Vespucci studied Columbus' maps, followed his route, and, by a whim of fate and the pen of a German geographer, Martinus Waldseemüller, gave his name, America, to the two western continents.

Europe seethed with excitement. Exploration and conquest were in the air. Nations vied with one another in fitting out expeditions to America. The Cabots touched the continent of North America (1497). Ponce de León discovered and named Florida (1513). De Piñedo mapped the coast of Texas (1519). Magellan's ship sailed round the world (1520–21). Cabeza de Vaca crossed the continent from Florida to the west coast of Mexico (1527–36). Jacques Cartier explored the Saint Lawrence River (1535). Coronado explored the Southwest (1540–42). Cabrillo named California (1542). De Soto (1541–42) marched through the swamps and forests of the Gulf country, slyly passed along from one Indian tribe to another by tales of glittering wealth that lay ever beyond.

Over the sea from Spain, Portugal, England, and France came explorers and gold seekers. It was the black-bearded Spaniards, however, who penetrated deepest into the country.

1. Explorers landing in the New World. 2. Columbus lands in the West Indies. 3. Spanish exploration of the Southwest.

And it was the Spaniards who introduced the horse to the Western World. The Conquistadores had brought horses to Mexico as early as 1519. Horses were part of the equipment of Ponce de León, of De Soto and the other explorers who landed in Florida. In Coronado's expedition through the Southwest there were one thousand horses. The Spanish horse, descendant of the fleet Arabian, left his own descendants on the American plains—the wild mustangs.

From the Florida coast armies of gold seekers struck inland. Indians were made to labor as guides and burden bearers. The only roads were Indian trails that threaded the forest from river ford to mountain pass. Indian dugout canoes, hollowed and shaped by fire from one huge tree, were seized for crossing broad streams. If no dugouts were available, nor materials for making rafts, and the current was uncommonly strong, horsemen formed a line across the river and received the full force of the water, thus enabling the foot soldiers to swim over in safety.

In the wake of the explorers came the settlers. French Huguenots, in 1564, made an attempt at colony founding on the Carolina coast, but it was doomed to destruction by the jealous Spaniards. Already Spain was massing ships and men to establish San Augustin on Florida's sunny sands, destined to be recorded in history as the first permanent white settlement in what is now the United States of America.

Chapter 2

SOLDIERS AND SETTLERS (1565-1606)

A caravel of 150 tons, a large galley propelled by oars and sail, several sloops, and the Governor's flagship, the splendid galleon San Palayo *of 600 tons burden.*

—FLORIDA RECORDS—*1565*

FOR NEARLY two months the ten Spanish ships had sailed west. Aboard were fifteen hundred men, women, and children, the colonists Governor Pedro Menéndez de Avilés was bringing to his new domain of Florida.

"Land! Land ho!"

Joyful voices echoed the lookout's cry. "Land at last. Blessed San Augustin be praised."

The coast of Terra Florida, that vast unknown country stretching northward from Mexico and westward from the Atlantic, was sighted on August 29, San Augustin's Day in the Spanish calendar. Eight days later the ships drew to shore. From dark holds crowded with military and agricultural stores, men and women swarmed up on deck, eager to catch a glimpse of this place that was to be their home.

All eyes stared at the line of golden sand, the fringed palm trees, and the low huts of an Indian village. Storm and sea-sickness and the fearful weeks of ocean tossing were forgotten in the thrill of this first look.

So great were the number of people and the amount of supplies that it took two days to land them. While naked Indians watched, anxiously but quietly, small boats plied from ship to shore, unloading bearded soldiers in polished helmets and half-armor, churchmen in cowl and robe, laborers in woolen jackets. Only when all others were ashore were the wives and their young ones landed.

Before the close of the second day, to peal of trumpets and boom of artillery salutes, Governor Menéndez disembarked in formal state, banners flying, his captains around him. Carrying a cross and chanting hymns of praise and thanksgiving, priests and people marched down to the shore to meet him, whereupon Menéndez, and his officers with him, knelt on the sand and kissed the cross. Then he took possession of the country in the name of the King of Spain; and all the officers swore a solemn oath of allegiance to him as their Commander General. After this a noble feast was served to which the Indians were invited. But the red men paid high for their first taste of wine and biscuit and quince preserves. Before night fell the Spaniards had taken over the Indians' village of bark huts for their own sleeping quarters.

To commemorate the day land was sighted, the new settlement was named San Augustin. By rule and measuring rope a town was laid out in streets and squares. Each family was given a town lot. Small rough houses were built. Tree trunks sharpened at both ends were planted upright to make a stockade.

Brass cannon were set up within this fort, with iron cannon balls and gunpowder stored close at hand.

Horses, cows, sheep, goats, hogs, and fowls had been sailed over in the ships. Hoes, spades, and plow irons had been brought; also seed for sowing fields and planting gardens, cuttings of grapevines, and slips of fruit trees. Among the colonists were twenty-seven families to till the soil. Of the eight hundred twenty soldiers many were also trained for such trades as tailor, carpenter, mason, miller, shoemaker, seaman, gardener, and barber. Negro slaves from Cuba were brought to plant sugar cane and manufacture sugar.

Each householder was given land for planting according to the size of his family. In these first hard years, however, there was more fighting than farming. For fear of the red-skinned savages, farmers dared not cultivate ground more than two hundred paces from the protection of the fort. The colony suffered a starving time. When the food they brought with them was gone, and the cattle and hogs were eaten or stolen by the Indians, many families had nothing to eat but palm berries and roots grubbed out of the marshes. All looked anxiously for the arrival of supply ships from Spain or Cuba. But a voyage to Spain and return took a whole year. To go to Cuba and back meant a month's sail. So the hunger pinch was often painful before fresh supplies came to hand.

For the men-at-arms there was the danger and excitement of exploring a new land. For their womenfolk there was the job of making a home in the wilderness. Daughters helped with the cooking, spinning, and sewing. Strong-shouldered boys were set to spading, planting, and cutting timber. An alert, keen-eyed lad might go on a map-making expedition with the Governor's surveyors. So valuable were these maps that they were sent back to Spain to be locked away from prying eyes. In fact, it was worth a man's life to show his map to anybody but a Spaniard. These heavily guarded secrets of trails, har-

bors, rivers were the keys by which Spain expected to unlock
the riches of her newly discovered lands.

Four priests arrived with the pioneers, and others followed
through the years. A church was built in San Augustin, and
the chaplain of the fort was often the *cura* or parish priest of
the town. In every home there would be a niche or shelf to
hold the image of some blessed saint. The christening of in-
fants called for festivities and gifts. Growing girls and boys
went to their first communion.

Religion, however, was often kept separated from a man's
deeds, for this was a cruel, bloody age. Human life and suffering were held cheap. Punishment of crime rested upon the
royal government. A written criminal code made legal such
tortures as lopping off noses, ears, fingers, and burning out
eyes. Beheading was a recognized form of execution, though
there is no record of any beheading in Florida.

The tiny outpost of empire that was San Augustin could
hardly be said to have prospered, but it persisted, finally rooted
itself firmly in the Florida sands. More acres were cleared and
planted. Fruit trees and vines from Spain came into bearing.
The Governor ordered a tract of woodland cut for timber,
and incidentally rid the settlement of a plague of mosquitoes.
An early historian describes San Augustin as "a little Town
without walls, built of wooden houses" and protected by a
wooden fort. Thus it stood in the year 1586 when the English
sea rover, Drake, arrived off the bar. He captured the fort and
the brass cannon, and the royal treasure chest full of silver and
gold. Drake burned the fort and the town and sailed away.
San Augustin rebuilt upon its ashes in enduring coquina stone.
By the end of the century its size was three squares in length
and four squares in width, with gardens to the west side, homes
close set together, a lookout and bell tower, a church, the
hermitage and school of the Franciscan Fathers, and a hospital
established for the poor soldiers of the garrison. By the year

WINGATE COLLEGE LIBRARY
WINGATE, N. C.

1. Bark house. 2. Stockade. 3. Sandglass. 4. Cartier on the St. Lawrence.

1606 the Governor could boast that his city contained one hundred twenty houses, not counting those of the Indians.

This same year Florida received its first visit from Bishop Altamirano, who had to dodge storms and pirates to cross the waters from Cuba. The Bishop confirmed 350 men, women, and children in San Augustin on Easter Sunday. Visiting each of the widely scattered mission stations, in three months he administered the rite of confirmation to 2,074 Indian converts.

Cart Wheels Rolling

Before the end of the sixteenth century a second Spanish colonizing venture had been undertaken. This was Don Juan de Oñate's *entrada* to New Mexico in 1598. Moving overland northward out of Mexico, he had with him four hundred colonists driving seven thousand head of horses, cattle, and sheep. With him too went holy friars in dark robes, and gentleman adventurers in gilded armor astride horses in trappings of blue and scarlet and gold. He had also a train of eighty-three carts loaded with food, arms, clothing—the first wheeled vehicles to rumble through our American history. Women trudged beside the carts where children too young to walk were perched atop the grain sacks.

The march started off, with embroidered banners flying and wooden wheels screeching on ungreased wooden axles. At a certain river crossing, these wheels made themselves useful in an unexpected way. Riders spurred their horses into the water, and men and boys goaded the cattle safely across. But the sheep almost drowned under the weight of their wet wool. To save his flocks, the leader ordered that the largest cart wheels be placed in the stream, rafts tied to them, and the whole overlaid with branches to make a bridge on which the sheep might cross over.

His first sight of the buffalo, the huge wild cattle of the

plains that were "bearded like billy goats and fleet as deer," suggested to the commander that crossbreeding with his own herds might produce a superior type of cattle. At his orders an enormous stockade was planted and mounted men went forth to round up the buffalo. But when the buffalo discovered the stockade, they stampeded so violently that the men would have been trampled to death had they not spurred their horses to a hilltop. Seeing that capture would not avail with such savage beasts, the Spaniards were forced to leave the buffalo undomesticated.

Battling against Indian tribes, crossing deserts and rivers, and pushing through mountain passes deep in snow, the great caravan slowly crept forward. A half year from the time they set out, the colonists halted in a captured Indian *pueblo* (town), which they renamed San Juan de Los Caballeros— that is to say, Saint John of the Gentlemen-on-Horseback.

The men who came with Oñate to New Mexico found neither the gold nor the jewels they had come to seek, but they did participate in great things. The leader and his scouts explored the land as far west as the Pacific Ocean, opened up a wide new region for Spain, and made contact with many Indian tribes.

Costume Contrasts

The Indians, so comfortably arrayed in tattooing, beads, and a feather, must have stared in amazement at the bearded men encased in clanking steel armor or swathed in cloth. These two extremes of costume had not the slightest effect upon each other. The redskins continued to be "face all over." The Spanish gentleman, whether in New Mexico or Florida, continued to outfit himself fashionably in corseted doublet, starched neck ruff, and trunk hose puffed out with buckram. His lady's garb was equally unbending, thanks to boned bodice over a wood-and-leather corset, buckram-lined bell-shaped skirt, and heavy overdress. Knitted stockings were something new and rare, and most people were satisfied with cloth hose cut on the bias to make them fit smooth. The Spanish cape, a great semicircle of velvet or woolen cloth, was the stylish wrap, and was worn by both men and women. And the wearer felt very fine indeed if he (or she) could top it with a velvet hat adorned with plumes.

Working folk's clothes were not so starched and stylish and were more comfortable. The farmer's leather doublet and woolen breeches, and his wife's linen headcloth, stuff bodice, and wide skirt, were the product of their joint labor in tanning hides into leather, shearing the wool from the backs of their sheep, growing the flax, spinning the thread, and weaving the cloth. A spinning wheel (said to be wondrous quick at twisting yarn) had been invented in Germany some years earlier, but few women owned such a wheel. All women, though, had been taught from girlhood to handle the ancient distaff and spindle. Boys and girls dressed like their parents. The babe in arms, victim of the belief that tiny limbs grow crooked unless held rigidly straight, was wrapped tight in swaddling clothes till half a year old.

A familiar figure about the settlement was the missionary friar in full-skirted gown of coarse wool, a rosary hanging from his knotted rope girdle, his bare feet stuck into leather sandals.

Each man-at-arms received an issue of clothing—a suit of doublet and breeches, a pair of coarse linen shirts, some short hose, shoes, hemp sandals, a hat, and a sword belt. Officers furnished their own armor, which consisted of steel breastplate, backplate, and helmet. The common soldier was provided with a canvas corselet wadded with cotton, which was considered ample protection against Indian flint-headed arrows.

The gentlemen-on-horseback rode up into New Mexico in plumed hats and velvet suits trimmed in gold and silver fringes. Those who walked went more soberly in cotton or wool or good stout leather. Alas, though, for gentlefolk's silks and working folk's leather: wilderness life ragged out the best of clothes, and all had to learn to patch and sew to keep their bodies covered.

Palm Thatch and Coquina

The New Mexican colonists did not build homes of their own for several years. They took possession of the mud-walled, flat-roofed Indian pueblos and made themselves as comfortable as possible with what household goods they'd been able to pack into the wheeled carts that followed the long trail northward.

Indian lodges also served the Spanish settlers in Florida as their first shelters. But as soon as the town was laid out men were set to cutting and sawing timbers. Small wooden houses were framed and quickly roofed in shaggy palm thatch.

Before the end of the century the Florida Spanish were building their homes of native stone. This stone they called *coquina*, meaning "shell," because it was made up of millions of tiny shells embedded in lime. At the quarry coquina was soft enough to be cut into blocks, but the air soon turned it hard. Negro and Indian slaves loaded the blocks on carry poles and lugged them to the building site. These early coquina houses were enormously thick of wall and solid of floor, the floors being made of coquina fragments tamped down in salt water. Roofs were palm-thatched or tiled in crushed coquina and oystershell lime moistened and shaped on wooden blocks. Houses were small; many of them contained only a main room or *sala*, a bedchamber, and a pantry. If a wooden second story were added, with a tiny window balcony, this upper apartment, according to Spanish usage, became the family living room. A dwelling erected about 1597, and purchased for the Governor's mansion in 1603, costing a thousand ducats, was evidently a house of considerable size.

Spanish-style furniture was large and heavy, ornamented with bold carving and hand-wrought iron. The Governor undoubtedly possessed a handsome table with hammered iron stretcher, a cabinet desk with iron hinges, a carved chair that was symbolic of his high position. He slept on a bedframe laced with rawhide thongs for springiness, and spread with a wool-stuffed mattress, pillows, and linen sheets. And quite likely he enjoyed such other luxuries as a mosquito netting of fine gauze, a tallow candle to burn in a brass *candelero*, and a sandglass to measure the time.

Sea chests were probably the only furniture most families fetched with them on the ship. But if father and the boys were handy with tools they could outfit the home with bunk beds like those the master carpenter built for the soldiers in the fort. Trees that had been cut down to clear the land were fashioned into board tables, benches, and low stools.

Because of the mildness of the Florida climate few houses were built with fireplace and chimney. A clay brazier fitted with an iron grille supplied warmth on a nippish morning, or a bed of coals for small cookery. The dome-shaped stone-and-clay oven stood in the yard. The great iron kettle swung above an outdoor fire.

Olla Podrida

> Pickled pork by the thousand pound,
> Honey put up in tubs so round,
> Strings of garlic, and good dried peas,
> Malaga raisins, biscuit, cheese,
> Pipes of flour, butts of wine,
> Quince preserves and comfits fine,

Vinegar, oil, mustard, and rice;
Here's every sort of food that's nice.

A good variety of tasty provisions were brought on the supply ships, but, alas, they were too quickly eaten up. The Florida housewife, struggling to keep her family well fed, found that most of her cooking was *olla podrida*—hodge-podge, a mixture of native and imported foods. When stirring up a vegetable stew she learned to substitute Indian maize and squash for Spanish chick-peas and onions. A porridge of maize meal was as filling as that made of Spanish wheat. To make little flat break-cakes, she could follow the Indian method from start to finish: soak corn in water. Heap the wetted grains upon the grinding-stone. Pound them to a paste. When the mixture is fine enough, take a lump in the hands, pat it thin, then lay on a hot stone to bake.

Cooking utensils fetched from Spain were few and precious. It was a proud woman who could boast an iron kettle, a copper bake pot, a long-handled iron stir spoon, and a knife for carving. A humbler sort of kitchenware could be had for the making—cook pots and water jars shaped of clay, gourds cut into dippers and bowls, wooden platters and wooden spoons. For crushing grain into bread flour, one could seek out a flat stone for a grinding block, and a smoothly rounded stone for a pounding pestle. If a housewife lacked a stone-and-clay oven in her yard, she could still bake bread in a covered pot set amid the hot coals. And fish could be soaked in olive oil, wrapped in leaves, and cooked under hot ashes.

Soldiers of the garrison were issued rations of biscuit, maize flour, jerked beef, wine, and olive oil. They complained that this was not enough when there were seven or eight children to be fed on the father's rations, so they begged an extra half ration for each small child, and for their daughters while they were too young to marry.

The *vino tinto*, a sour red wine for daily use in place of

drinking water, was more important to the Spaniard than his bread and meat, and huge casks of wine were sailed in from Spain. Olive oil was imported to use both for seasoning and for frying. If olive oil was not to be had, a very good oil could be extracted from native nuts by crushing nut meats and salt together in a mortar, then squeezing the mixture through a cloth till the oil came out.

By 1579 the Governor of Florida was able to report: "There are beginning to be many of the fruits of Spain, such as figs, oranges, pomegranates, and grapes. Also beans, melons, pumpkins, lettuce, onions, and garlic. This land raises sugar cane well."

America was not lacking in food products of her own. Sweet scuppernong grapes, squash, maize, persimmon, and mulberry were native. Rivers teemed with fish. The woods abounded with squirrels, rabbits, deer, partridges. The *gallipavo* (peafowl), as the Spaniards dubbed the splendid bronze-feathered turkey of the Western World, was delicious meat whether roasted on a spit before the fire, or fried in oil well seasoned with wine and spices.

Barber Surgeons

The eating of strange foods, change of climate, accidents, and Indian arrows caused considerable suffering among the Spanish colonists. At such times they turned to the barber surgeon stationed at the fort to clip hair and trim beards, but who was also supplied, according to European custom, with a "case of instruments for making cures." The barber surgeon's first treatment for practically any ailment from a pain in the head to pimples on the face was a bloodletting—to pop a lancet into the patient and draw off a basin of blood. After an Indian battle, or a clash with English pirates, there was full need of the medico's skill. With nothing to relieve agony of pain (save a chip of wood for the wounded hero to clamp teeth on to prevent him from biting off his own tongue), he extracted spear splinters, treated burns, probed for bullets and arrow points. His instruments included needles and catgut thread, forceps, knives, and a saw with which to amputate a limb.

Along with the battle casualties there were sicknesses that struck both the soldiers in the fort and the families in the town. Through the "drinking of raw waters and sleeping in the dews" folks fell into bone-shaking agues and scorching fevers. (Florida was plagued with mosquitoes, but not for three hundred years were mosquitoes to be blamed for malaria.) Fortunately there was help right at hand. From watching how the Indians cured themselves with native herbs and shrubs, the Spaniards undertook to work their own cures with these same medicines of "great virtue". A tea brewed from the pleasant-tasting sassafras root was esteemed to drive away the fever: a bit of sassafras being chewed and left in the hole of an aching tooth "doth most marvelously quiet the pain."

The following remedy traveled all the way from America to Europe to be written down in a *Booke of Physick:*

For The Cold Stomach Ache:
Take Tobaco Leaves, warm them well in hot ashes and apply externally. The more ashes that stick to the leaf the better the remedie worketh and the more strong the effect.

To pound the green tobacco leaves into a healing poultice, to beat the little round knobs of nut grass roots into a spicy-tasting powder to comfort the stomach—these methods and many other medical matters the Spaniards were happy to learn from the Indians.

Latin in the Wilderness

On the other hand, some very unwilling little Indian boys were the first pupils in the new church schools founded by the Spanish. The red men had their own ideas on education, quite practical ideas. Boys were taught to track the wild woods creatures, to look for trail sign, to chip stone axes and arrow points, and to bend wood into bows. Girls were taught to shape pots of clay, to weave baskets, to tan hides. The Spanish idea was entirely different: the small savages must come to school "to learn to read and learn the doctrine of Christianity."

In 1573 Spanish friars of the Franciscan order founded a monastery in San Augustin. Twenty years later these same brave and pious brown-robed men had spread out into the wilderness, built little churches, and opened schools. Twice daily the bell called their young pupils to the school to memorize prayers and sing hymns. As the church service was in the Latin language, the little Indians singsonged the prayers and hymns in Latin too.

The children of the Spanish settlers were also instructed in "Christian doctrine". A girl's education seldom went beyond this religious training and what her mother could teach her of cooking, spinning, sewing. A few boys went on to reading in both Spanish and Latin; still fewer bothered to learn to write. For those who did undertake writing, the first lesson was how to cut a goose quill into a pen, and how to make ink by dissolving ink powder in water. As both ink powder and blocks of white paper had to be sailed from Spain, writing equipment was scarce and costly.

By the beginning of the seventeenth century higher education was receiving its due in Florida through a classical or Latin school established at San Augustin by the Franciscans. Latin was the language of the Church. It was also a language in which learned men of every European country could speak their ideas to one another; hence Latin was a necessity to a priest, and a great convenience to any man in public life. A boy attended Latin school from his seventh to his fifteenth year, during which period he was thoroughly dosed on Latin grammar and reading from the Latin classic authors. Even when he sat down to dinner he had to listen to scholarly reading. There was no lack of rules to guide his deportment in school. He must sit straight upon the bench, fix his look upon the teacher, and listen well to his words. If a boy were naughty, or merely careless, he promptly learned the sting of the stick vigorously applied where it would do the most good.

Books of Romance Banned

Very few books were brought to Florida. Indeed, few of the settlers, other than priests and public officials, could read. Under order of the King of Spain, the romantic books so popular throughout Europe—the tales of enchanted castles, fire-breathing dragons, brave knights, and fair ladies—could not be sent to the colonies. His Majesty was of the opinion that such light reading would waste time that could much better be put to discovering new lands and building new forts. But there was reading matter. Every brown-robed friar who risked his life to open a mission church in the Florida wilderness carried with him a Bible, a missal, and other devotional books. Also, there were the books for study and reading aloud in the school.

By the end of the sixteenth century both Florida and New Mexico had produced books written within their borders. A Franciscan friar, known as Brother Domingo Augustin, translated a catechism and grammar into the Florida Indian language called Gualean. And Captain Gaspar de Villagra, one of the gentlemen-on-horseback who rode so splendidly clad in velvet suit and plumed hat, wrote a poetical account of the great overland colonizing expedition in which he took part. He titled his book the *Historia de la Nueva Mexico*.

Fiesta

The Spanish settlers might live happily enough without reading, but entertainment was a necessity. Festivals were celebrated with enthusiasm. The historian of the conquest of New Mexico tells that the colonists, on their long and dangerous journey, made frequent pauses for rest and enjoyment. Any event, from the safe crossing of a great river to the subduing of an Indian tribe, might be the occasion for a *fiesta*. One time a whole week was spent in celebrations. There were horse races, bullfights, a mock battle in which soldiers clad in armor and mounted on horses fought against each other with blunted lances and swords. Other young gallants, all handsomely dressed, displayed their skill at horsemanship by casting a lance through a small ring while riding at full speed.

To these same New Mexican colonists goes the honor of the first dramas written and acted in what is now the United States. When they took possession of the new country, the soldiers acted in two dramas composed especially for the occasion. One was a comedy to set the audience to laughing. The other was a religious pageant that showed the coming of the Christian priests, the Indians greeting them with joy and being baptized in large numbers.

Across the continent in Florida festival days were marked by religious processions and church services. Then the crowd scattered to enjoy the holiday in feasting, sports, and card games.

By royal edict, gaming at cards and dice was forbidden in the colonies. A Florida official, however, requested permission to lift the ban in the garrison, saying that cardplaying was the usual pastime of soldiers and made them stay quiet in the fort. The gamesters had to depend on cards fetched from Spain, or use homemade ones cut out of old parchment drumheads.

The cards were brightly painted in red, blue, and yellow. The four suits were named *Copas* (cups), *Espados* (swords), *Bastos* (clubs), and *Oros* (gold coins). A popular sixteenth-century card game was *El Hombre,* in which he who undertook to name the trump said, "*Yo soy el hombre*" ("I am the man"), and thus must defend his bid or lose the game. In this period when few people could read and still fewer could write, score was kept by counters, which might be small pebbles, shells, or even beans.

To the Spaniard dancing seemed as natural as walking. Young and old enjoyed the lively stamp and whirl. If music of flute and drum was lacking, the singing and hand-clapping of onlookers beat a rhythm for the dancers. The strutting *pavana* took both name and steps from the *pavo* or peacock. Partners stood side by side in a line, all facing the same way, and moved forward in time to the music. Especially enthusiastic dancers sometimes indulged in the movement known as "the leap," which was done with both feet off the ground and raised in the air. This was described as being "very lively".

Boys and girls had their singing and dancing games in which they circled and marched and wove in and out under uplifted arms. They also had lively, romping games, such as *El Burro* (the donkey), in which the players took partners, then all joined hands and danced around a lone player who was called the donkey. At a signal each player grabbed a new partner, and the one left partnerless became the donkey.

Equipment for a game of *Tenis* (tennis) was quite simple— a length of rope and a ball. Rules of play were simple too. Players batted the ball with the palms of their hands back and forth across the stretched rope. The ball must be returned while in flight, or after the first bounce. To send the ball under the rope was a fault.

Guessing games were a quieter pastime. A favorite was to

try to guess how many beans or maize kernels an opponent held in his tightly closed fist.

From the young redskins the young Spaniards could copy such fun as the Indian stick game, where four small sticks, painted on one side, were tossed into the air, and a point counted for each stick that fell painted side up. In the Indian ring game, a ring of bone or wood was thrown upward and the player strove to catch it on a sharpened stick.

Singing and Playing of Instruments

One thing that the Spaniard did not borrow from the Indian was his music. The primitive rhythms of the redskins' song, accompanied by flutes, drums, and rattles, beat harshly on the Spanish ear. The Spaniards, however, had plenty of music of their own. It is recorded that when Governor Menéndez came to Florida, he marched at the head of his guardsmen to the music of "two pipers and drummers, three trumpeters, a harp, a violin, and a psaltery." At a feast given by the Governor, music was played and some of the gentlemen "sang in concert." One of the Franciscan friars who journeyed up into New Mexico was a musician. He built a small organ for the first chapel, and trained a choir of Indian singers.

Many a song of Old Spain came to New Spain in the hearts and memories of the colonists who dared cross the wild waters to found new homes in the wilderness. They brought solemn Latin chants for church ceremonials, and melodious *cantigas* or carols in praise of Our Lady and the Blessed Saints. Cradle-songs and work songs and love songs crossed the ocean. A pioneer mother crooned her baby to sleep to the same ditty her mother had sung to her. A man pulling oars on a Florida river or herding cattle across the plains of New Mexico forgot his weariness in song. A lover separated from his sweetheart

tunefully implored the swift-winged swallow "to fly my heart
to where my loved one waits."

Everybody loved to sing the catchy tunes and numerous
verses of the ballads that celebrated brave knights and battles
in the long and bloody war between Christian Spain and the
Moorish invaders, a war that was finally fought to Spanish
triumph in the very year that Columbus rediscovered the
Western World. A favorite among these ballads was "The
Moorish King's Lament", in which the enemy cries out his
grief over the loss of his royal city of Alhama.

> Sound the hollow drums of war,
> Beat the loud alarm afar;
> Tell that Christians, stern and bold,
> Have obtain'd Alhama's hold.
>   Woe is me, Alhama.

Chapter 3

THE HOME-BUILDERS (1607-1699)

They burrow themselves into the Earth for their first shelter under some Hill side, casting the Earth aloft upon Timber; they make a smoky Fire against the Earth at its highest side.
—THE WONDER-WORKING PROVIDENCE

"HEAVE HO! Up—up with it!"

A tall boy in leather doublet and baggy breeches put his shoulder to the log and pushed with all his might. Grunting and sweating, he strove beside the men as they planted the palisade of tree trunks. The little cave dug into the hill slope must be safely walled in before nightfall.

On the bleak New England shore the women and girls huddled together. Behind them lay long, weary weeks of

29

wind-tossed crossing of the gray Atlantic. Dumped on the
ground around them were piles of tools—shovels, spades, plow
irons, sickles for cutting the grain not yet planted, axes for
clearing the land, double-handled crosscut saws for shaping
the timber into shelters. Before them loomed the vast forest
that was to be conquered with these bits of iron, a forest
haunted by wolf howls and red Indian whoops.

The year 1607 had seen the founding of Jamestown, Virginia. The leader, Captain John Smith, wrote: "We had fifty-
two gentlemen adventurers besides the preacher and two surgeons. Also four carpenters, twelve laborers, a blacksmith, a
sailor, a bricklayer, a mason, a tailor, a drummer, four boys,
and some others." A hundred and four colonists to found the
first permanent English settlement in the Western World—
and not a woman in the lot. Gold, and raw materials for
England's trade—such was the dream. The reality was starvation, sickness, and hostile savages. A tobacco patch planted in
1612 shaped the course of Virginia's destiny. Here was a
money crop, one that demanded a wide acreage. As men scattered from the town, the plantation system got its start. Wives
arrived to join their adventuring husbands; in 1619 a bride
ship sailed to port. This same year saw the House of Bur-
gesses, the first representative assembly in America, sitting in
the log church at Jamestown. Twenty Negro slaves, unloaded
from a Dutch man-of-war, were eagerly bought by the tobacco planters.

In 1620 the little ship *Mayflower* landed another English
colony far to the northward at Plymouth Bay. This pilgrim
band of men and women had crossed the ocean not to hunt for
gold but to seek religious and civil freedom. In 1630 Governor
John Winthrop landed at Boston Harbor with eight hundred
colonists. New England began to fill up with small towns and
villages, each with "a broad street crossed midway by another
street, and houses of good hewn plank standing in their own

gardens." Here the township was the unit, with voting in town meeting restricted to church membership.

Through the years English-speaking people continued to pour into America, founding settlements in Maryland and Pennsylvania and on the coasts of Carolina.

Wherever they settled, these transplanted Englishmen reckoned by the same money they had in England—pounds, shillings, pence. And they suffered the same lack of gold and silver coins. Of necessity they swapped corn for salt, tobacco for a silk hood. They paid reverence to rank, reserving to the big landowner or rich merchant or to the minister and his lady the honored titles of Mister and Mistress. Lesser folk they addressed as Goodman and Goodwife or Goody. Laws were strict and punishments harsh. Petty wrongdoers were fastened head and hands in the pillory, and pelted with rotten eggs. The more hardened criminal was set astride an instrument of torture known as the "wooden horse", and a weight of iron attached to each foot so that the sharp-edged plank would be more painful. The ducking stool was the special reward of gossips. Witches were condemned to death. Even so, belief in witches continued to send shivery thrills down people's spines. Indeed, it was a common belief that the Evil Eye soured the ale, and that hags on broomsticks dried the milk cows, mildewed the barley, and made children cross-eyed.

Law and religion went hand in hand. Fines were collected for Sabbath-breaking, that is, for swearing, playing games, or taking journeys on the Lord's Day. Ministers preached two-hour sermons, and old and young had to go to church or meetinghouse, or be put in the pillory and risk hell-fire.

At the age of sixteen a boy legally entered manhood, took on the burden of taxes, served in the militia. Girls married at sixteen or younger. But before there could be any wedding, the banns or notice of intention to wed must be published three times at Sunday service or town meeting.

This was a time when big families were a treasure. Many hands were needed to wrest a living from the land. Tiny toddlers were set to shelling beans and hulling corn. The older girls lent a hand at knitting the family's stockings, making clothes, dipping candles, boiling soap, cooking meals, smoking, salting, and drying foods for future use. The big boys walked behind the heavy ox-drawn plows, scattered the seeds, swung the chopping hoes. At harvest time they helped thresh the grain and winnow the chaff. They could turn a hand, too, to boat-building, and assist at the vats where hides, laid down in oak bark and water, were tanned for the family's leather boots, breeches, and doublets.

Boys liked to go on a tramp with the men to the coast to fetch bags of salt made by boiling sea water in a pan till the water evaporated and the coarse, dark salt was left. Even more exciting was exploration of the swampy lowlands for bog iron. It was a proud boy who lugged home a big lump of the soft, spongy metal for the ironmaster to smelt into bar iron in his crude hole-in-the-ground furnace, then mold into tools or plow irons or good strong cook pots.

While the first English colonists were getting settled, a group of sturdy, pipe-smoking Dutchmen, their red-petti-coated *vrouws* (wives), and rosy-cheeked children, arrived in 1626 to plant farms and do fur trading along the Hudson River. They bought Manhattan Island from the Indians for twenty-four dollars' worth of beads, tiny metal mirrors, and other trinkets. Their village of New Amsterdam, on the southernmost tip of the island, speedily grew into a town. Because of its magnificent harbor this bit of New World Holland attracted an odd mixture of nationalities. Its population was well peppered with Spaniards, Germans, French, Swedes, Turks, Jews, and Italians, and, on occasion, as many as eighteen languages could be heard being spoken in its bustling market place. Presently, however, England and Holland got into a war; a strong English fleet sailed into the harbor, demanded the surrender of the town, and changed its name to New York.

In 1638 a Swedish ship sailed up the Delaware River and landed a band of colonists. From the French settlements in Canada French explorers began moving south through chains of lakes and streams, and on down the Mississippi River, laying claim to territorial possessions in the great river valley. In Florida and the Spanish Southwest, soldiers, settlers, and teaching friars were holding the land for their king. As many as ninety flourishing mission stations were established in New Mexico alone.

Each European colony planted in America had to go through its own period of terrible first years. These were desperate years, darkened by sickness, starvation, Indian fear. Yet, somehow, men managed to build shelters for their families; they built churches in which to worship God, and log forts for protection from redskins on the warpath.

Every year more ships brought more people across the ocean. Before mid-century Plymouth Colony boasted nine towns, and Massachusetts Colony had grown to a population of sixteen thousand. In another quarter century Virginia could count fifty thousand inhabitants. Philadelphia, getting off to a late start, was in 1682 a hamlet of three or four cottages; by the end of the century it was a city of ten thousand souls, and could boast a "Noble Town House, Handsome Market House and Convenient Prison, also Grew Houses, Bake Houses, and several good Schools." Boston, a metropolis of seven thousand, took precautionary measures against fire by ordering every householder to have a hogshead well filled with water near his door. New York, that had been New Amsterdam, began flaunting street lights "in the dark of the moon for the ease of the inhabitants"—said lights consisting of a candle in a lantern hung out on a pole at every seventh house. And every town that deserved the name protected its citizens by a night watch "to walk two by two from nine o'clock till break of day," carrying rattle and staff, calling the hour and the weather, and "preventing mischief."

Gabled Roofs and Tall Chimneys

First shelters had been caves dug into a hillside, or bramble huts roofed in sod, with fires on the dirt floor and smoke holes above. As soon as possible, better homes were built. The Dutch on Manhattan Island made themselves cozy in brick or stone dwellings with crow-stepped gable turned to the street. The English erected sturdy framed houses, that is, wooden houses with their wall timbers framed or pegged together on the ground and then pushed up into place by neighborly man-power. Walls were covered with clapboards handsawn in the saw pit. Steeply pitched roofs were thatched in reeds cut from the marshes. Up under the roof was a narrow loft chamber where the older children slept. The downstairs room, known as the hall, the kitchen, or the keeping-room, was where the family worked, cooked, ate, and where many of them slept. Household activities centered about the fireplace with its cheerful blaze and the great iron pot swinging from the lug pole.

Clocks were scarce, so people learned to tell time by the sun. Wax candles, being costly to buy and a lot of trouble to make, were saved for special occasions, and most families got along with a smoky, smelly Betty lamp, which was simply a shallow iron bowl holding a tow wick floating in fish oil. To light the lamp one struck a spark with flint-and-steel or lifted a glowing ember from the hearth fire.

There wasn't much furniture. The great chair, carved of solid oak, with tall back and stout stretchers to brace the legs, was reserved for the man of the house, or for the preacher

1. New England clapboard house. 2. Dutch house. 3. Stocks for public punishment. 4. Table chair. 5. Great bed and trundle bed.

when he came to visit. The rest of the family sat on benches or stools, with sometimes a cushion to make the sitting less hard. Chests did duty as seats, tables, and storage place for clothes and household linens. Another space saver was the table chair—a large chair with the back hinged to be let down on the arms as a table. In one corner of the room stood the great bedstead, its four tall posts almost touching the ceiling, its curtains snugly draped to keep out the cold. Here father and mother and one or two of the younger children slept, with baby in a cradle close by, where mother could put out her hand and set the cradle to rocking. If the family was very large—and most families were large in colonial days—there'd be a low trundle bed on rollers to pull out from under the big bed.

As the colonists prospered they built bigger houses with more rooms—"ye great Hall, ye Parlor, parlor chamber, great chamber, small chamber, ye loft chamber." A kitchen, placed off in the yard to lessen danger from fire, was flanked by such outbuildings as a dairy springhouse, dovecot, smokehouse, brewhouse, weaving house, tool house, hen house, stables, and barns. These new dwellings followed the familiar style of peaked roof and tall chimney. That is, the Dutch and English colonists kept to this style, for that was the way houses were built in their old homelands across the sea. But men from other countries had other ways of building. The Swedes along the Delaware River put up log houses with the logs laid one on top of the other instead of standing on end as the English had stockaded their first shelters. And the Spanish in New Mexico combined Indian and Spanish ideas in low, thick-walled dwellings with walls of sun-dried clay bricks called *adobes*, and a flat roof of clay supported on heavy beams and close-laid crossbeams. Hot-weather cooking and other work were done in a shady courtyard or patio at the rear.

Baked, Boiled, and Brewed

In most of the colonies, cooking was an indoor job done above a bed of coals in the fireplace. The big pots swung from an iron crane across the wide mouth of the chimney. Three-legged skillets and bake kettles stood on the hearth amid the hot ashes. Often a joint of meat dangled on a spit before the blaze, with a child standing by to turn it slowly about till the meat browned on every side and good gravy ran down into the drip pan.

This was the time when Americans got the habit of having meat on their tables three times a day if they felt like it. In Europe poor people thought themselves lucky to get a bit of meat once a week, but matters were different in this new land. If father was busy at the plow, a couple of boys might go into the woods with his gun and likely enough come back with a turkey gobbler, a brace of pigeons, or even a fat buck. Meat kept for future use was laid down in the "powder trough", that is, laid down in salt. Sides and joints were smoked over a hickory fire. Or the housewife, her wide petticoats looped up out of the way and a protecting apron tied about her middle, vigorously wielded chopping knife and wooden mallet to make sausage that she seasoned with sage and thyme and marjoram from her own garden.

The colonists were accustomed to eating wheat and rye bread, but they learned to eat the golden Indian maize, and to cook it in many ways. They made it into Hasty Pudding by "stirring meal and water with a snack of salt and boiling it in a pot." They made Rye-and-Injun, a dark, coarse, but tasty loaf, mixed of rye flour and Indian corn, and baked in the brick oven built into the same chimney with the fireplace.

A few cattle were brought over at an early date. "A cow to every six persons, and two goats to ye same." Thereafter milk, butter, and cheese were enjoyed along with the bread and meat.

Vegetable gardens were planted. Apple trees and peach trees were planted and brought forth fruit. And children seldom needed urging to go into the woods and fields and gather wild plums, nuts, persimmons, and strawberries.

Having to drink water was one of the sorest trials the colonists had to put up with. If water didn't actually "rust the stomach," at least it had a bad reputation for unhealthfulness, and much time and labor were spent making more pleasant-tasting thirst quenchers. The Spaniards pressed grapes into wine. The English and Dutch experimented with brewing beer and ale from various grains and fruits. Persimmon beer turned out to be a favorite in some places. Toward the end of the seventeenth century, imported chocolate and tea were served in small cups, but only the rich could afford such costly drinks.

Grown-ups sat at table on long benches. Children often had to stand behind their elders and eat what was passed back to them. Meat was served on a big pewter platter. People ate from wooden trenchers or pewter plates. Wooden noggins, earthenware mugs, or pewter or silver tankards held the drink. The table was spread with a home-woven linen "board-cloth". Napkins were plentiful, and necessarily so, for though forks were just coming into use, it was still mannerly to eat with the fingers.

Ride and Tie

Tasty food and a snug house were good reasons for staying at home. Indeed, traveling was such a troublesome undertaking that people didn't go gadding any more than they had to. All remembered the terrors of the voyage that had brought them across the ocean—the howling tempests, the threat of pirate attack, the fear of lying becalmed till ship's timbers rotted and everyone sank to a watery death. They had endured two months and more of crowding together in a dark hold under a ceiling so low that a tall man could scarcely stand upright. Cooking was done on a square of bricked hearth on deck. When waves rolled high there could be no cooking at all, and passengers gnawed stale biscuit or were too seasick to eat. A fair day, though, brought everyone on deck to enjoy God's blessed sunshine, to watch the porpoises leap and the gulls flying overhead.

A few Indian trails threaded the forests but there were no roads that could be called roads. Travelers rode horseback or walked, for wheeled carts couldn't squeeze between the trees edging the narrow paths. Often there were not enough horses when several members of a family needed to travel, so then they rode "ride-and-tie". One person bestrode the saddle and another sat behind on a pillion or flat cushion; this couple cantered off, and another couple walked. After a mile or so, the riders dismounted and tied the horse to a tree; they walked, while their companions got a chance to ride. Thus four people, by taking turns, made very good time on one horse.

The easiest way to travel was to follow the rivers and creeks in a dugout canoe, or to sail along the coast in a tiny sailboat. Because of this, many families built their houses close to water.

Although wheeled vehicles were scarce in the Atlantic colonies, in the Spanish Southwest the rumbling of wheels and squealing of axles of the *carros del Ray*, the King's wagons, moving in a long, dusty line out of Mexico up to the mission outposts of New Mexico, could now be heard. Once in every three years a great caravan of thirty wagons and five hundred mules would bring in supplies of food and clothing, and people going to and from the province were thankful to travel under its armed protection, although the caravan took six months to creep northward across mountains and rivers.

When journey's end was sighted, the lead team was decorated with banners, and the caravan swept into the mission yard amid shouts of welcome.

Farthingale Fashions

"Thrum—thrum—thrum," whirred the spinning wheel as a girl in wide skirts and white linen kerchief stepped to and fro, twisting a fluff of soft wool into strong thread. "Thump—thump—thump," pounded the loom as mother wove wool and flax thread into linsey-woolsey cloth to be cut and sewed into warm coats and petticoats.

Folks hankering for style, and able to pay for it, sent back orders to Europe for garments of velvet and damask. Most families dressed in homespun—made of flax grown in the home field, of wool sheared from the family sheep and colored by dyes concocted at home by steeping certain roots and barks in water. Oak bark made a useful brown, barberry root a yellow, indigo a blue, and pokeberry juice boiled with alum a splendid crimson. "One pair scissors and a few needles" were household treasures. Cutting out by guess, or using a ripped-up garment for a pattern, home seamstresses laboriously hand-stitched the new clothes.

Fashion was much the same in all the colonies. Stylish dames appeared in starched neck ruff and farthingale petticoats, the farthingale being a bolster-shaped wool-stuffed cushion tied about the hips to hold out the skirts. Gentlemen were equally grand in cartwheel ruff and farthingale breeches, that is, baggy breeches padded to puff them out. The doublet, which was a close-fitting garment worn by both men and women, was ornamented with slashes to show the bright-colored lining. Boys and girls were as starched and padded as their elders. Indeed, one good thing about this overstuffed style was that garments wadded with wool offered some protection against Indian arrows.

Gentlemen paid considerable attention to their hair—to long, curling locks on the head—and to the trimmed and starched beard on the chin. A poet of the period wrote:

> The soldier-beard doth march in shear'd
> In figure like a spade,
> With which he'll make his enemies quake,
> And think their graves are made.

Before the mid-seventeenth century the ruff and farthingale disappeared. And not long after that the masculine outfit of doublet and knee breeches became the three-piece suit of coat, waistcoat, and breeches. It was about this time, too, that men shaved off their beards. They shaved the hair off their heads and put on wigs with long curls spread over their shoulders. Boys also put on wigs. In summer the wigs were so hot and uncomfortable that they were often laid aside and a cloth cap worn instead. Women didn't bother with wigs. They wore white "coifs" or caps, and folded a white linen kerchief about their necks.

At this time few soldiers had suits of steel armor, but all were supplied with stout leather jerkins or "buff coats"—so called because the first ones were made of buffalo hide.

Bitter Doses

Every family that could afford it had brought a medicine chest stocked with "Spirits of Castor, Syrup of Saffron, and Purging Pills." Sickness struck so hard that before many months were past the chests were emptied of their medicines. Mothers of ailing children, whether the disorder be "ye ricketts, fitts, or ye chin-coff" (whooping cough), turned in desperation to concocting teas, bitters, and soothing ointments from herb recipes passed from goodwife to goodwife. In small kettles swung above the hearth fire, they brewed wormwood for bellyache, pennyroyal for sniffles, sarsaparilla for a blood purifier. A bit of iron, filed to a powder and mixed in a syrup, made an effective tonic for pale faces. Boys and girls squirmed and backed off from the bitter doses held to their lips, but they didn't mind climbing up to gather cobwebs from the dark corners of the loft room, for everyone knew that to stop bleeding there was nothing better than a handful of cobwebs bound over the cut.

Several doctors were among the early colonists, but these learned and expensive gentlemen were mainly called in to set broken bones, sew up a dangerous sword wound, or to let blood. Phlebotomy or bloodletting was the universal cure that let out the disease from the body.

A doctor's surgical equipment was scanty—"knives for lancing abscesses and trimming wounds, forceps, probes, needles, a dismembering saw." If an arm or leg had to be cut off, the doctor had nothing stronger than an opium powder or herb drink to soothe the pain. The suffering during an amputation was dreadful, almost beyond endurance. The patient was roped to a table. Men gripped his wrists and ankles to hold him down. The doctor cut with what speed he could while the injured man screamed and prayed.

Sanitary laws were passed by government officials, and under threat of public whipping at the whipping post, people were forbidden "to wash unclene linnen, pot or pann within twentie foote of ye Well or Pumpe." Still the settlements suffered outbreaks of "Feavers and Bloody Flux" (typhoid). They also suffered from "ye cold in the head" and toothache. Most dreaded of all sicknesses, though, was the smallpox that periodically took its death toll. Doctors could do nothing to prevent it and little to cure it. About once in every generation an epidemic of smallpox would sweep through a settlement, leaving new graves in the churchyard. The faces of persons who survived were often hideously pock-marked, but at least they were safe from a second attack.

Dame School

Unlike sickness which struck at high and low alike, the enjoyments of book learning were for the privileged few. Most folks had to be content with learning the catechism, a bit of reading from the Bible, and how to work. Under the apprentice system poor boys and girls were "bound out" to work for a master or mistress a certain number of years, receiving in return food, shelter, and instruction in the employer's trade, be it blacksmithing, farming, or housewifery.

Little ones learned their letters at dame school, which was usually kept in some good dame's kitchen so that she could cook, spin, and hear lessons all at the same time. The room was noisy with the buzz of small voices blabbing the syllables— "b–a, ba; b–e, be; b–i, bi; b–o, bo; b–u, bu," and on through the alphabet, it being cherished opinion handed down from times past that lessons recited the loudest were remembered longest. Chief standby of the dame school was the hornbook, which wasn't a book at all, but a paddle-shaped board to which was tacked a piece of paper protected from sticky fingers by a sheet of transparent horn. The letters of the alphabet were printed on the paper, as well as the Lord's Prayer, and the numbers one to ten. A primer combined reading lessons with religion in such verses as: "In Adam's fall, We sinned all." Girls were taught to knit and do plain sewing. To be able to read the Bible, count eggs and knitting stitches, and reckon small money was considered quite enough book learning for a female.

A boy who planned to go into business when he became a man went to a schoolmaster to learn to write and to cypher, that is, to do arithmetic. The schoolmaster held forth in a one-room schoolhouse furnished with a desk and chair for himself, with backless benches and a "rod of correction" for his scholars. Paper was folded and hand-sewn to make a "copie book" for the writing lesson, and a "cyphering book" into which arithmetic problems and solutions were transcribed with laborious neatness. School often kept six days a week the year around.

Families of wealth who desired to give their sons a classical education sent them abroad to study, or a bond servant "that hath been brought up in Latin" might be purchased as a tutor. Or the boys were sent to Latin school.

In all the colonies there was a beginning of schools. In the Spanish Southwest brown-robed friars at adobe-walled missions gathered in the Indian children to teach them Christian doctrine and handicrafts. In Virginia in 1634, a public-spirited gentleman donated "200 acres and eight cows and their milk and increase" for the maintenance of a "free schoole". On Dutch Manhattan, by the year 1638, there was a school "supported out of the public monies." A Latin school was started in 1652. New England attended to the serious business of opening schools early. Massachusetts in 1647 enacted a law that every township of fifty householders should appoint "one within their towns to teach all such children as shal resort to him to write and read," his wages to be paid "eithr by ye parents or by ye inhabitants in general." (*All*, of course, meant all boys. But everyone knew this.) Twelve years earlier, in 1635, Boston had opened a Latin school where boys memorized grammar and read Caesar and Cicero in Latin.

Two colleges were founded in colonial America in the seventeenth century—Harvard in Massachusetts, in 1636, and William and Mary in Virginia, in 1693. As the chief object of each was the training of a "learned and godly" ministry, much attention was paid to reading the Old Testament in Hebrew and the New Testament in Greek.

On the Bookshelf

Reading was not a popular pastime. Books were few and hard to get, and not everyone knew how to read. After a toilsome day behind the plow or at the loom, it was not easy for eyes to follow print by the blaze of the hearth fire or the dim glow of a Betty lamp. Still, colonial America was not bare of books. Bible and catechism stood on every family bookshelf. The minister, being learned as well as godly, had these books and others. Rich gentlemen owned libraries of a hundred or more volumes—religious books, and books of law, medicine, and history, of Greek and Roman poetry and mythology.

The Bay Psalm Book, printed in 1639, has the honor of being the first book published in English America. The first American newspaper, *Publick Occurrences*, appeared in Boston in 1690, but it died after a single issue. People still had to depend on getting their news by word of mouth.

Sometimes a man or woman who had been taken captive by the Indians, and later rescued, wrote a narrative of adventures among the savages. Both grown-ups and youngsters read these thin pamphlets with thrills of excitement.

Such ancient tales as "Jack-the-Giant-Killer" and "Hop-o'-My-Thumb" might be heard when the family gathered round the hearth fire, but there were no storybooks especially for children. People believed that reading should be for instruction, never for entertainment. Even *Aesop's Fables*, with its talking animals and birds, was a textbook in Latin school. Late in the century, however, a wonderful book came to the colonies. This was John Bunyan's religious allegory, *Pilgrim's Progress*. Here, for the first time, were instruction and enter-

tainment combined. Readers breathlessly followed the pilgrim's adventurous journey to the celestial city.

To make these books and others more readily available, the
first public library in North America was founded at Charleston, South Carolina, in 1698.

Homemade Fun

Colonial legislators were much given to enacting restraints
upon the fun-making of their more lively neighbors. In every
colony laws were passed rebuking those "who spend their time
idlie by day or night playing at dice and cards." Gaming at
Ticktack was prohibited during the hours of church service,
along with such frivolities as "Dancing, Playing at Ball, Bowl-
ing, taking Jaunts in Boats and Wagons."

Many parents were of the belief that "Satan lurked in idle
play." Even so, children managed to snatch moments of fun
between their chores of picking up chips and scattering grain
to the fowls. Small boys played soldier, marching and drilling
with stick guns. Small girls set up housekeeping under a shady
tree. Most toys were homemade. A little mother would happily sew petticoats and caps for a rag baby fashioned from
scraps of linen stuffed with wool, its cheeks stained a beautiful
red with berry juice. Balls were made of bits of leather stitched
into shape and stuffed with hair. The proud possessor of a
pocketknife could cut willow twigs into whistles and canes
into flutes. If marbles were lacking, boys could still play Roll-
the-Hole by using nuts to shoot at the mark, and the lucky
lad had the fun of eating his winnings. Romping games, such
as Leapfrog, Blindman's Buff, and Prisoner's Base called only
for nimble legs and arms and cheerful whoops.

The game of Loggats demanded no more equipment than
a bundle of loggats (sticks) and a stake set up as a mark. Each
in turn hurled his loggat at the stake, and that player won

whose loggat came closest to the stake without knocking it down.

Another sport that required only simple equipment was Stool Ball. "Two do play at Stool Ball. Set up a stool for the one to bowl at. The other player stands beside the stool and striveth to turn the ball away with his hands. If the ball strike the stool the players change places."

Any holiday saw young men and boys testing their skill and strength in wrestling and foot racing. Youths and maidens gaily bowed, turned, and swung their partners as they stepped a reel or round to some old ballad tune.

Merrie Tunes and Solemn Psalms

The songs of their old homeland were the only songs the early colonists knew. Mothers rocked their babies to the same lullabies they had heard as children. "Trip a trop a trover, the cows are in the clover"—and on through endless verses about piggy in the bean patch, the calf in the meadow, ducks in the water, and so "goe to sleepe my little one." When young people met together they joined voices in the old familiar airs. They tunefully bewailed the cruelty of "Barbara Allen" who scorned the love of young Jemmy when he "on his deathbed lay." In merrier mood they sang the rollicking song, "To-morrow the Fox Will Come to Town":

> I must desire you neighbors all,
> To hallo the Fox out of the Hall,
> And cry as loud as you can call:
> Whoop, whoop, whoop, whoop, whoop,
> O keep you all well there.

There were musicians and musical instruments in Virginia at an early date. Drums and trumpets were used to gather men from work or to call them churchward. In the Spanish-held lands there was no lack of musical instruments. In the adobe-walled missions, Spanish friars not only taught their Indian converts to sing and play, but to make their instruments, even organs. "It is to praise the Lord to see in so short a time so many chapels with organ-chant."

Stern New Englanders frowned upon musical instruments in their meetinghouses; but psalms were sung, the deacon starting them off. Lack of enough psalm books to go around made it necessary for the deacon to line out the words—that is, read aloud a line at a time, pause for the congregation to sing it, then read another line. In those dangerous pioneer days, how comforting it was to hear the deacon's firm voice lining out the beloved Twenty-third Psalm:

> The Lord to mee a Shepheard is;
> Want therefore shal not I.
> He in the folds of tender grasse
> Doth cause mee down to lie.

Chapter 4

FRONTIERS OF FORTUNE (1700-1763)

The Land is a good Land, supplied with Timber for building. The fatness of the soil flourishes Fruit, Corn, Indigo, Tobacco—often two crops to the year. Here an Ox can be raised with as little expense as a Hen is raised in Europe.
—LETTERS FROM EARLY COLONISTS

LAND-HUNGRY people swarmed across the ocean. Gentlemen in velvet coats and silver knee buckles. Workmen in leather jackets and worsted breeches. Single men, and men with their wives and children. Free men, and bond servants who were bound over for a period of years to work out the cost of their passage over. Englishmen came, Scotsmen and Scotch-Irish, German Palatinates, French Huguenots, Welsh, a few Swedes and Dutch. From an overcrowded Old World they poured in a swelling tide to the Virginia and Maryland of the spreading tobacco plantations and few towns, to New England with its close-knit townships and thriving industries, to New York, snatched from the Dutch, to Penn's Quaker colony of Pennsylvania and its great law guaranteeing civil and religious freedom, to Carolina of the sea island plantations with the port of Charleston as its heart. Clerks in colonial land offices dipped goose-quill pens in ink and wrote orders for government surveyors to "admeasure out land for these who have arriv'd to plant and inhabit the Province."

Still the people came. The French founded Mobile and New Orleans on the Gulf coast, and claimed for their King Louis the vast Louisiana territory of the Mississippi River basin. To counter this French thrust down the center of the continent, the Spanish erected great fortress missions on the Texas plains. With the settling of a group of Canary Islanders at San Antonio, the best traditions of Spanish family life were brought to the wilds of Texas.

Old World rivalries flared in the new land. Spain had joined France against England, so Spaniards in Florida joined Louisianian French and Canadian French against whatever English colonial settlement lay nearest. Each side stirred up its redskinned allies against the other side. Dwellers on outlying farms and plantations fled from the horrors of Indian torch and massacre to the more protected towns. When the war danger was past, they returned to rebuild burned homes, put seed in the ground, round up strayed cattle.

Most people's living came from the land through farming and livestock raising. A successful farmer produced enough for home needs and a surplus for marketing. Every big plantation was a small world complete in itself, weaving its own cloth, smithing its own iron tools, grinding grain between its own millstones, hewing and sawing timber for its dwellings and outbuildings. Tobacco and rice fields made a man rich; what kept him so was raising the corn, beef, pork, and fowls for family eating and for feeding the steadily increasing number of black slaves. Landowners bought workers from sea captains who were doing a thriving trade transporting Negroes from Africa and exhibiting them for sale at the spring and autumn fairs. From then on it was the new master's responsibility to teach the jungle savages to wear clothes, speak a few words of English, do useful labor. The planter's ideal was to "keep a good house, live bravely, and be worthy of much honor"—a splendid existence, but certainly not an idle one. He must provide shelter and food for all who looked to him. Within his person must be united various trades and wide knowledge: he must be a farmer to know how to plant and harvest profitably, an engineer to be able to ditch and drain the land, and a carpenter to erect dwellings, barns, cribs; often he must be a boatbuilder, a wheelwright, and a cooper to barrel the crops; and always he must be a bookkeeper to balance the account books. The plantation mistress must be equally diligent in directing her maids in the house, the kitchen, the dairy; and hers was the task of dosing her family and servants when any were ailing.

By sweat on their brows and calluses on their palms, men wrested a living from land, forest, and sea. Fishing and salt-making were two industries that went hand in hand, the freshly-cleaned fish being rubbed with salt and spread out to dry in wind and sun. Where there were pine forests men "burned" tar for waterproofing the seams of ships and boats. Lumbering, besides furnishing timbers and clapboards for houses, supplied tall pine masts and oak planking for ship-building. Conveniently close to the shipyard would be a long, narrow ropewalk with a great spinning wheel at one end, and maybe a half-dozen men and women walking slowly backward and forward as they twisted hemp fibers into strong cordage for the rigging of ships. Vessels from colonial ship-yards carried cargoes of tobacco, rice, hides, tar, pitch, and fine furs. On the return trip came silver plate, silks, wines—rich prizes for Blackbeard and the other greedy pirates who harassed the shipping lanes.

Men with trades, such as weavers, glovers, tanners, saddlers, shoemakers, flocked to the towns. Such industries were largely in the home, and children worked with their parents, or were "bound out" to learn some other trade. It was a proud father that could boast of a son apprenticed to a hatter, another to a printer or a doctor, and daughters helping in the shop, the ropewalk, the kitchen.

Towns were growing into cities, with Philadelphia (population twenty thousand) queen of them all. Improved night-watch systems made an effort to combat footpads and violence. Volunteer fire-fighting companies bought hand-pumped engines. A few blocks of paved street offered riders in coach and wagon the excitement of nearly jolting their teeth out bumping over cobblestones instead of sitting bogged down in mud. At a handsome town hall the provincial court sat in state, and bewigged gentlemen and hoop-skirted ladies danced at the assembly. And it was a backward city indeed that did not have a printing shop and weekly newspaper.

Each passing year saw the country growing richer. In cities and on the plantations there was a show of magnificence. Splendid mansions were built and furnished with mahogany sofas and brocade draperies. Tables were set with silverware and sparkling wines. Fashionable costumes demanded such costly items as silken hose, silver buckles, hair powder and pomade. The labor of a horde of servants was required to keep these lordly few in style and comfort.

The Spanish Southwest had its aristocracy of great landowners entitled to the honored address of *Don* and *Doña*. French Louisiana had its royal officials. The English colonies had their own men of authority and wealth who sat high in Church and Assembly. Colonial planters, merchants, and ship-

Poor Richard, 1733
AN
Almanack
For the Year of Christ
1733,

1. Early colonial building. 2. Mahogany tall clock. 3. Silver candelabrum. 4. Chaise.

builders along with acquiring fortunes were getting a taste for fine manners. Emphasis was on "genteel behavior"—particularly for females. The fair sex must walk mincingly and sit rigidly erect. Girls suffered hours of anguish strapped to a backboard to insure that admired posture. Dancing masters were engaged to teach young ladies to curtsy and young gentlemen to bow with hand over heart. Children were trained to address their elders as "Honored Sir" and "Honored Madam".

Girls married young. To reach the age of twenty years and still be unwed was to be dubbed an old maid. Among families of wealth a marriage was ofttimes arranged by the parents. No matter how a heart might ache for a lost love, a father's command must be obeyed. In French Louisiana the bride's dowry was a matter for family conferences. In Spanish Texas the love-smitten *caballero* was expected to furnish his ladylove's trousseau, perhaps even making a trip to far-away Mexico City to bring back a small trunk filled with feminine finery. In the English colonies, the "thrice published banns" were becoming outmoded. It was more stylish to wed by special King's license.

Weddings were occasions of festivity, with the feasting, drinking, and dancing lasting three days or a week. Funerals were also social gatherings that called for a lavish spread of food and drink. The King's birthnight was generally celebrated with a splendid ball, with supper at midnight and dancing till dawn.

The punishment of evildoers was a public spectacle. The whipping post stood on the main street of every town so that the sight of a bare back being lashed till the blood ran might serve as a warning to others. Pirates, murderers, and horse thieves were hanged. Men who could not pay their debts were locked up in the jailhouse where the public funds fed

them for twenty days; thereafter whoever had them im-
prisoned must feed them.

The mid-eighteenth century was hardly past when Spain
and France and England were again at each other's throats.
Again colonial America echoed the turmoils of Europe: war
in the South—the Florida Spanish fleet attacking Georgia; war
in the North—the French and Indian War spreading terror
and desolation.

Nationally speaking, much colonial property changed
ownership during these fateful years. English victory cost
France her hopes of an American empire: France ceded
Canada to England, handed over Louisiana to Spain. England
had captured Spain's rich island of Cuba; for the return of
Cuba, Spain, who had owned Florida for two and a half
centuries, ceded the Land of Flowers to victorious England.
Now came a time of sad upheaval for many Floridians. Rather
than live under an alien rule, whole families packed their
household treasures and took ship for Cuba. On their departure
the very name of their historic city, San Augustin, was
Anglicized to Saint Augustine.

While she was losing an old colony, Spain was founding a
new one—California on the far Pacific coast. Soldiers, colonists, and priests were sent northward from Mexico in 1769
to plant a mission at San Diego among friendly Indians. In the
next few years other mission settlements were established.
These strong, thick-walled structures that formed one side of
a quadrangular stockade were part church and part fortress.

In the eastern part of the continent people were on the move
too. Victory over the French had opened up the back country
to the English-speaking colonials. In crowded coast settlements, men poor in this world's goods shouldered gun, axe,
and bag of seed and set out over the mountains to the fertile
lands of the Ohio Valley.

Dinner at Four O'Clock

There wasn't much danger of starving for any pioneer
family that had energy enough to plant a field, aim a gun, or
drop a fishing line. The French who came to Louisiana wrote
glowingly to their friends across the ocean: "We live on wild
beef, wild turkeys, ducks, quail. Peaches and figs are in
such abundance that we make preserves. We also eat water-
melon and oranges and the pineapple, which is the most ex-
cellent of all fruits." New Englanders stored apples for winter
eating, made pumpkins into pies. Beans layered down with fat
meat in an earthen pot were left overnight in the brick oven
to bake to tender toothsomeness. A vegetable much appreciated in the southern colonies was the sweet potato. Roasted
in hot ashes till it was soft and sweet, the potatoes tasted "like
chestnuts, only better."

Girls early learned from their mothers to bake breads, buns,
puddings, pies, and loaf cakes. Colonial cake was no whimsy
of whipped-up batter poured into a pan, but was shaped of
solid bread dough yeast-raised and enriched with eggs, butter,
sugar, and fruit. Reprints of popular English cookbooks were
offered for sale in the provinces, but recipes were mostly
handed down by word of mouth, and measurements were
vague: take a handful of dried fruit, butter the size of an
egg, as much spice as will sit upon the point of a knife.

In well-to-do city homes and in the great plantation mansions, food was spread with a lavish hand. A supper party
might include in its meat courses beefsteak pie, ham garnished
with cloves, a chicken fricassee, turtle with saffron and rice.
The sweet course served whipped sillabub, trifles, jams, jellies,
and cake. Drinks were wine, ale, cider, and punch. An old
recipe for punch states that "every host of fashion hath a
punch bowl of wrought silver on his serving table. Every

dinner is preceded by a drink of punch blended of wine, water, sugar, and lemon, sprinkl'd o'er with grated nutmeg."

The stylish hour for dinner was four o'clock in the afternoon. Probably the hour was set this late to allow time to prepare the elaborate foods. Kitchen equipment, however, had some recent improvements to help speed the hands of the cook. In addition to the bricked oven, the kettles hanging from the crane in the fireplace, and the usual three-legged skillets and covered bake pots that stood amid the ashes, there were now long-handled toasters and waffle irons. Finest of all was the tin "roasting kitchen"—a large metal box with front open to the blaze and a tiny door at back, through which one could reach to baste the meat as it browned to tender juiciness.

To enjoy a sip of chocolate, one purchased cocoa beans from which to prepare the chocolate drink. Coffee beans were roasted and ground in the home kitchen. Every town market had tea for sale—and how the ladies loved their fragrant tea. What pride they took in the tea table's fragile china cups, the silver teapot and sugar tongs.

Colonial Mansions

As the colonists prospered, their prosperity was reflected in their homes. A gentleman lived in a mansion if his house had both front and back stairs—the back stairs indicating servants and wealth and style in his manner of living. Rich merchants and plantation owners built splendid red brick mansions with hip roofs and a trim of white stone around the front door. That American invention, the up-and-down-sliding sash window, now began to take the place of the hinged casement window. Rooms were large, square, high-ceilinged, with paneled walls. Floor plans showed a spacious arrangement of "drawing room, dining room, card room, bed chambers, and a central stair-hall." A narrow, enclosed stair led from base-

ment kitchen to dining room, or a small serving pantry inter-
vened if the kitchen were set off in the yard.

The heavy carved oak furniture of the early colonists was
replaced by mahogany in the new Queen Anne style with its
graceful curved legs, or by the still newer straight-legged
Chinese Chippendale style ornamented with inlay and lacquer.
Beds were made of mahogany too—tall four-posters complete
with bed steps by which one climbed in. A dressing box with
two tiny drawers under a framed mirror, and designed to
stand on the bedchamber chest of drawers, was a necessity to
a lady. For wig-wearing gentlemen, an appropriate item was
a wig stand, with a drawer for pomade and hair powder, and
a curved top on which to rest the wig in its off moments.

Foreign luxuries were unloaded from tall-masted ships. For
people who had no taste for paneled walls, there were gold-
flecked flock papers and Chinese rice papers painted with
bright birds and flowers. From an assortment of "week clocks,
month clocks, quarter chime clocks" one could pick a time-
piece and have it put into a tall mahogany or lacquered case.

Splendid silver graced the dining rooms of the rich, but the
usual tableware was pewter, with a full set of dishes and plates,
termed a "garnish of pewter". For the tea table, that center of
social chat and graces, there were tea sets of delicate china-
ware.

Instead of the ancient smoky saucer lamp there was now the
elegance of silver candlesticks holding perfumed bayberry
candles. Or spermaceti candles "each brighter than three tallow candles" gleamed in rock-crystal lusters hung from the
ceiling.

Bouncing Hooped Petticoats

> Let your gown be a sacque, blue, yellow or green,
> And frizzle your elbows with ruffles sixteen;

Make your petticoats short that a hoop 8 yds wide
May decently show how your garters are tied.

Thus they sang to the Age of Elegance, to frivolous fashions and mincing manners, to hoop-skirted ladies and hand-
kissing gallants.

Workaday costume was plain and practical. Laboring men
went soberly in knitted cap or felt hat, in leather jacket, canvas
breeches, yarn hose, and heavy leather shoes. The goodwife
did her housework in homespun petticoat, woolen bodice,
wide apron, and a linen kerchief folded about the shoulders.
But folks who could afford to do so followed fashion with
vigor. Every ship that sailed to Europe bore anxiously penned
measurements for plush coats and brocade mantles, for gowns
of China silk and India print, for silk ribbons and gold and
silver lace.

A stylish gentleman favored silk for hose and knee breeches,
for embroidered waistcoat and flaring coat. But his ruffled
shirt must be of fine white linen, his cravat of white lawn
edged in lace. The crowning glory of masculine costume was
the wig. This mass of false hair (costly to buy and costly to
keep curled and powdered) was so heavy that many a fine
fellow found it more comfortable to carry his hat in his hand
than on his head. But what was comfort compared to fashion?
Gradually the full wig, with curls hanging over the shoulders,
gave place to a smaller wig with a queue tied at the back of the
neck.

At first, ladies dressed their hair small and smooth under
ruffled caps. But during the passing years, it worked up to a
gigantic hair-do of false locks spread over wire frames and
wool pads, the whole plentifully dusted with white powder.
At the same time skirts grew fuller and fuller, until finally
somebody invented the hoop skirt or whalebone petticoat to
hold out the skirt.

Children were dressed like "little ladies" and "little gentle-men". Small girls, their waists pinched in tight bodices, bil-lowed about in hoops. Small boys in knee breeches, flared coats, and ruffled shirts had their hair cut off and powdered wigs put on their heads.

Polite Accomplishments

Private schools put notices in the newspapers to inform parents that their sons and daughters might be "Accommo-dated with Boarding" and exposed to an amazing assortment of polite accomplishments, such as "Vocal and Instrumental Musick, Dancing, Reading with Elegance and Propriety, Epistolary Writing, Drawing and Water-Painting." Espe-cially for the young ladies was instruction in "Quill-Work, Feather-Work, Shell-Work and Flowers for the Head." And for the young gentlemen, "all the Attitudes and Positions peculiar to the Art of Fencing"; also Horsemanship, "an Art justly admired and counted part of Polite Education."

Only boys went to Latin school. And only boys, of course, went to college. Registration inducted the college freshman into a daily routine of rising by the bell, study, recitations. All games and sports were forbidden as waste of time. A tutor for each class gave instruction in every subject during the four-year course, putting emphasis on Latin, Greek, and theology.

The town schoolhouse was also strictly masculine. The long backless benches were closely packed with boys, small ones to the front, tall ones to the rear. Reading, spelling, and the catechism were "blabbed" in loud whispers. Only the master had a printed arithmetic book, and the boys copied the prob-lems into their homemade "cyphering-books". Writing lessons were reserved for the big boys. Any boy who was slow "to speak up" or who wiggled about got a sharp whack over the knuckles.

Rich merchants and planters sent their daughters to the expensive private schools to learn reading, writing, fine manners, and fancy needlework, to tinkle the harpsichord and step the minuet in the genteelest fashion. At dame school, poor girls learned to read and sew and count on their fingers, and that was judged schooling enough for them.

The Penny Merriments

Religious books and solemn histories and the Greek and Latin classical authors filled the home bookshelf. Young readers were provided with *The Naughty Boy Reformed* and *The Dying Words of Hannah Hill aged 11 Years*. But now there was also a beginning of storybooks for children. Tiny books no bigger than the palm of one's hand, covered in gay colored paper and illustrated with woodcut pictures, were carried by peddlers going about the country with packs on their backs. These little books sold for a penny, so people called them "penny merriments"; and children loved them. Some were printed versions of the ancient tales, "Tom Thumb" and "Robin Goodfellow". Some were abridgments of adventure tales written for grown-ups, such as *Gulliver's Travels* and *Robinson Crusoe*. Out of the peddler's pack came *The Puzzling Cap*, which was a book of riddles. *The Little Pretty Pocket Book* was filled from cover to cover with rhymed rules for playing games. The *Mother Goose Melodies* set young tongues to singsonging happy nonsense about cats and fiddles and cows that jumped over the moon. Even so, it was not the intention of parents that young people should read only for fun. To every verse and story was added a moral lesson to "make a little Boy wise and a little Girl good."

In several towns groups of book-minded young men organized library societies. They would put their money together and order a box of books from abroad; gradually other books were bought, a room found to shelter them, a plan devised for lending—and a library society was born. Mingled with the volumes of essays, history, and poetry were some of the new English novels. But many people considered novel-reading frivolous, if not downright sinful.

Every town of any size had its weekly newspaper. On four small pages were spread "the latest foreign advices" and such local news as the hanging of a pirate, text of a sermon, marriage and death notices. Merchants advertised "Chintzes and Calicoes", schoolmasters gave notice of classes in "Dancing, Musick and Needlework", and rewards were offered for return of runaway apprentices and bond servants.

The first magazine published in the colonies was the *American Magazine*, issued at Philadelphia in 1741. Others followed, but few survived for as long as a year. These magazines or "literary storehouses" tried to cram a little of everything into their thirty to sixty small pages:

> Old-fashioned writings, and Select Essays,
> Queer Notions, Useful Hints, Extracts from Plays,
> Relations wonderful, and Psalm and Song,
> Good Sense, Wit, Humor, Morals, all dingdong,
> Poems and Speeches, Politicks and News,
> What some will like and some refuse.

Smallpox Parties

Next to the Bible, the family's "book of physick" was probably the best-read volume in any household. Woodall's *Surgeon's Mate* told plainly "ye exact cure of wounds made by gun shot or otherwise." Of more general use was the book on herb medicines. With Culpepper's *Dispensatory* in hand, mother could flip through the pages and learn how to make a poultice of "Bark of Slippery Elm", how to brew a "Sweating Dose" of the dittany plant, and how to make a "Comfortable Juleb for a Fever" out of white wine and barely water mixed with barberry conserves.

Doctors believed in generous dosing, handed out pills as big as the end of one's thumb, bitters by the cupful. The respected title of "Doctor" indicated no soft and easy life. Most medicos started out as apprentices to physicians, and, by the actual doing, learned to set broken bones, probe for bullets, prescribe medicines. Acting as their own druggists, they rolled pills and pounded herbs, between bedside visits. There were few hospitals, and these offered little beside a bed to lie on, and some man or woman to give medicines, provide food, wash linens, and keep an eye on the sick.

The terrible scream of "Mad dog! Mad dog!" froze the blood in people's veins. In spite of the doctor's slashing knife and the searing of the wound with a red-hot iron, nine out of ten victims of mad-dog bite died of the choking horror, hydrophobia.

But with smallpox it was a different story. Something was being done to take the terror out of the once fatal smallpox epidemics, for in 1721 inoculation for smallpox was introduced into America. A doctor would take a drop of pus from a pimple on a smallpox patient and rub it into a tiny cut on the arm of the one to be inoculated. This would give the new patient a made-to-order case of smallpox which was usually very mild, seldom left any pockmarks, and forever protected him from having the disease again, no matter how often exposed to it. Seemingly, people everywhere would have rushed to avail themselves of this protection, but they did not. Because this treatment came from far-off Asia, ignorant persons denounced it as a "heathen rite that could never succeed on Christian bodies." The first American doctor to practice inoculation was taken from his home by a mob and whipped. But when inoculation was approved by men of wealth and importance, it suddenly became so fashionable that everybody

who could afford it wanted to go to one of the "stylish Inoculation Farms" where, in company with friends, they could
be "sowed with the smallpox" together, break out in fever
and pimples together, and get well together. Young ladies
usually carried along some pretty clothes, for one never could
tell when one might catch a beau during the weeks of companionship at a "Smallpox Party".

Horse Bells and Riding Chairs

The jingle of horse bells meant a pack train was on the
move. America still had few roads, and most of these were
bad, so much of the country's produce was carried by pack
trains over narrow trails called "tote-roads." People living on
the frontier made up caravans of horses laden with skins and
furs, and journeyed in to civilized parts to trade their wares
for iron and salt and a bit of luxury. In the long-settled regions
where there were roads, even though rough and muddy,
strong wagons with canvas-covered tops were the freight
carriers.

People who went on lengthy trips encountered many varie-
ties of transportation along the way. Perhaps the first lap of the
journey would be aboard a ship sailing down the coast. Next
might come travel on foot, on horseback, or on the hard
wooden bench of a springless stage wagon, with stops at a
roadside tavern for meals and a bed. If the traveler made a
connection with a stage boat he could continue on down the
flowing road of a river, and sleep as he rode—that is, if he
brought his own blanket to spread on the bunk shelf.

Ships from colonial shipyards—splendid two-masted brigs
and three-masted barks with canvas swelling in the wind—
were sweeping down the sea lanes, loaded with cargoes of rice
and furs and tobacco for the European markets. A ship sailed

to the destination of its cargo, and passengers went along if they so desired. There was nothing even remotely resembling a regular transoceanic passenger service. If he needed to make a sea journey, the colonial traveler scanned the weekly newspapers for notices of sailings. Even after his passage was booked with the captain, he more often than not sat cooling his heels at a tavern while the ship tarried a day or two longer to pick up more goods.

Friends who lived in different parts of the country seldom wrote to each other unless they knew of someone going traveling who would carry the letter. In 1717 an overland postal route was established between Massachusetts Colony and Virginia, the postrider requiring one month in summer and two months in winter for his trip on horseback. There were no postage stamps, and one paid the postrider three pence or six pence or even a shilling if the letter had to travel a long way.

Only families of wealth owned a great four-wheeled round-bottomed coach with the coachman's high seat up front and four horses in the harness. Handsomely painted and cushioned, and bouncing along on curved iron springs, the coach was a splendid sight. But it was so monstrously heavy that it was forever getting stuck in mudholes. Much more useful was the riding chair or chaise, a two-wheeler with a seat wide enough for two passengers, and light enough for one horse to pull.

The Governor's Ball

The grandest social event in any colony was the Governor's ball. Lanterns were held high by servingmen, and street crowds gathered to watch, as coaches and sedan chairs deposited guests at the door of the mansion. Ladies in plumed headdresses and gentlemen in powdered wigs were ushered in to make their bow before the Governor and his lady, then back stiffly away, for none might turn a back upon the king's man.

The music began a stately beat, three crotchets to the bar. The ball opened with a minuet—slow, elegant, elaborate. As important as the dance movements were the bowing, posing, kissing of hands. The steps, from whence came the name, were all *minuet*—small, dainty, mincing. Later, to lilt of fiddles and flutes, came the lively gavotte, a quadrille, a reel, each dancer showing the polishing effects of select dancing schools by graceful glide and pointed toe. Supper was served at midnight.

Race week, when country gentry came to town and fortunes were won or lost on the fleetness of a horse, was a favorite time for balls. Floors were waxed for dancing, and whist tables were set up for the chaperoning dowagers.

Such lively fun as "a pair of silver buckles to be wrestled for, a greased pole climbed, a slippery pig caught," as well as goods to buy and barter, brought people together at the spring and autumn trade fairs. Another sociable time was training day, when the young men gathered for drill. Roll of drums and the captain's shout "By platoons, march!" brought family folk up on tiptoes to watch their boys train with the militia. After the drill came contests in running, jumping, wrestling, boxing. Best of all was the target shooting, where to "thread the needle" meant putting a bullet through a hole in a plank, and "snuff the candle" meant firing a ball through a far-off candle flame without quenching it. Adding to the fun, there might be a limber-legged tumbler or a Punch and Judy puppet show. And always there was a fiddler to saw out dance tunes so that light-heeled youths and maidens might gaily step rounds, jigs, and hornpipes.

Children were no longer entirely dependent on homemade fun. Shopkeepers advertised toys for sale, "Wax Dolls, Singing Tops, Marbles, Balls," and also board games such as checkers and backgammon. A little book with rhymed rules for playing games had this advice to offer on playing marbles:

> Knuckle down to your Taw,
>   Aim well, shoot away;
> Keep out of the Ring
>   And you'll soon learn to play.

Gather Round the Harpsichord

Young voices blended with the melody of the harpsichord. Song followed song, the trilly "la–la–la–la" of "The Lass with the Delicate Air", the lively beat of "The Girl I Left behind Me", and that stirring tribute to ships and sailors, "Heart of Oak."

Just as gentlemanly accomplishments included the art of playing the flute, so must a lady know how to finger the harpsichord. Handsomely decorated in gilt and carving, the harpsichord was a fitting piece of furniture for an elegant parlor. Pressure on its ivory keys produced small, sweet sounds as accompaniment to ballad singing. But there were hours of toil that must precede those tinkled tunes, as small girls in bouncing hoop petticoats and ruffled caps counted their "one–two—one–two" and laboriously fingered keys in music lessons.

To the horror of solemn psalm-singers, but to the delight of those whose pulse beat in rhythm to a merry tune, were ballad operas imported from England. Here were old folk tunes dressed up with new words. For sociable singing, there was nothing so good as "Old King Cole" who called for his pipe, his bowl, and his fiddlers three; unless, of course, it was the catchy "Sally in Our Alley":

> Of all the girls that are so smart,
>   There's none like pretty Sally.
> She is the darling of my heart,
>   And lives in our alley.

Trained voices sounded in French Louisiana. In 1728 a nun of the Ursuline convent in New Orleans could report that "on Easter Sunday we sang motets in four parts; and on Low Sunday we sang the entire Mass in music."

New Mexico churches had enjoyed organ music for nearly a hundred years by the time the first organ was brought to the Atlantic colonies—to Pennsylvania in 1703. In New England the "godly viol", or cello, was now permitted to accompany church singing and keep the devout from going astray on their psalm tunes.

Music not only gave pleasure but served useful purposes as well. Singing lent rhythmic swing to the hand that pushed a broom, to brawny arms that rolled logs and piled stones. When neighbors worked together at "raising" a church, barn or dwelling, a lively tune helped lift the timbers into place. In this age of careful chaperoning, when courtship must be carried on with an older member of the family present, music was ever an ally to youthful love-making. So round the harpsichord let us gather while eyes speak their tender message and lips warble tunefully:

> Sweet Nellie, my heart's delight,
> Be loving and do not slight
> The proffer I make,
> For modesty's sake;
> I honor your beauty bright.

Chapter 5

LET FREEDOM RING (1763-99)

Give me Liberty or give me Death.
                    —PATRICK HENRY, 1765

VICTORY BONFIRES flared in all thirteen of the English colonies. The Peace of Paris had been signed in 1763, and the horrors of the French and Indian War were at an end. The French had been driven out; the English held America eastward from the Mississippi River.

Boys rushed about whooping, and throwing on more pine wood. Girls clapped their hands to see the flames leap up. Men and women joined their voices in the victory songs.

Alas, the colonists found such joyful celebrations sadly premature. They had exchanged, it seemed, a threatened French oppression for a very real English oppression. Mother England thriftily planned to make them pay for the French war she had just won. America must sell her rice, furs, tar, all her raw produce, only to England. America must buy naught but English manufactured goods. America must make nothing for herself which English manufacturers desired to sell—she must not weave a yard of fine woolen cloth nor shape an iron pot. America must affix a tax stamp on all law and business documents, on all pamphlets and newspapers, and must pay a tax on tea.

But America thought otherwise. The years of bloody struggle had united the scattered English-speaking settlements, had trained thousands of resolute men in the use of arms. "No taxation without representation" roared the colonists. "Down with tyranny! Give me liberty or give me death!"

On April 19, 1775, Minute Men rushed to defend the village of Lexington, Massachusetts, from a body of red-coated troops.

On July 4, 1776, the Liberty Bell clanged its iron-tongued shout for freedom. "Long live our new nation! Long live the United States of America!" The Declaration of Independence spoke out for all the world to hear:

"We hold these truths to be self-evident: that all men are created equal; that they are endowed by their Creator with certain inalienable rights; that among these are life, liberty, and the pursuit of happiness."

But this was only the beginning. Between the glad pealing of the bell and hard-won freedom stretched the seven long years of the Revolutionary War. England had no intention of giving up her profitable colonies; English armies invaded the land. The Americans fought back: under General Washington's command, trained militiamen in blue-and-buff, farmers with flintlock muskets snatched from above the fireplace, frontiersmen carrying the long, slender, American-made rifles that were to make history, swarmed to meet the invader. Battles in the north were fought: Trenton, Brandywine, Saratoga; battles in the south: Fort Moultrie, Savannah, King's Mountain. Thousands of Washington's soldiers were killed in the fighting, thousands died of the camp fevers, but other thousands took their places and the war went on.

Farm lands were ravaged by Tories who wanted England to win, houses were burned, families fled as refugees from their homes; still the war went on.

But help was on the way. A French fleet sailed into American waters. The valiant young Marquis de Lafayette unsheathed his sword in the cause of freedom. Then Yorktown, in 1781, and victory.

With victory, the American Revolution had brought the American people the right to make their own government, to follow their own religion, to think their own thoughts, to speak out and fear no man. The thirteen colonies—Connecticut, Delaware, Maryland, Massachusetts, New Hampshire, New Jersey, New York, North Carolina, Pennsylvania, Rhode Island, Virginia, South Carolina, and Georgia—had become thirteen American states. They had their freedom, but their new nation had no head; it had only a congress that lacked any real power. This Congress might pass useful laws but could not compel obedience to them; it might ask for money, but could not force the furnishing of it; it might demand soldiers for defense, but could not draft them. The states—each with its own interests and without the bond of war to unite them—fell into quarrels and suspicions of each other. Thousands of Americans in 1787 thought it was important to keep out any other state's worthless paper money. It was also necessary to keep an eye on boundary lines which a neighboring state might try to push back on a dark night. Not a very favorable climate, certainly, for the forming of a constitution and a strong national government.

And yet it happened: the miracle of patriotism and common sense prevailed over provincialism. Politicians, businessmen, farmers, lawyers, rose above themselves to establish a constitutional government, and made possible the greatest democracy in the world. General George Washington, the idol of his country, in 1789 made a triumphal trip from his Virginia plantation home, to New York, to be inaugurated as first President.

Three new states were admitted: Vermont in 1791, Kentucky in 1792, and Tennessee in 1796. The South, that had been overrun by the enemy, was rebuilding its profitable agriculture. Because of embargoes on rum and whale oil, New England was turning from shipping to manufacturing. The territory just over the mountains to the west was booming. Men were moving in to take up bounty lands given in payment for army services. They came by wagon and pack train, they built boats and floated down rivers. Every state on the Atlantic coast felt the drain of families moving away to the West.

Of course, this lustily growing United States of America wasn't the whole of the American continent. Florida, which had been under British domination for twenty years, was ceded back to Spain. Across the continent in California, Spanish friars in huge stone missions were instructing the Indians in crafts and Christian doctrine. Louisiana was prospering under its new Spanish rule. In New Orleans a handsome stone cathedral and a *cabildo* (government house) were erected. Sugar mills and spreading cane fields were bringing wealth to the plantations. Comfortable in her French-Spanish existence, Louisiana looked uneasily at the ever-increasing hordes of English-speaking frontiersmen barging hides and furs and timber down the Mississippi River.

In frontier homes, and in the old settlements, women breathed a prayer of thankfulness for peace and went on about their work. There were many things to keep a woman's hands busy. Milk must be set to cool in the springhouse, churned into butter, or pressed into cheese. The vegetable garden must be planted according to the "moon signs" in the almanac. Hens must be set on the approved number of eggs; goose feathers dried to stuff feather beds and pillows; wing feathers laid aside to be shaped into writing quills. Spring was the time for boiling soap. An autumn duty was candle-dipping, to insure a sufficiency of firm white candles to light the longest and darkest winter night.

There were a few factories with clumsy hand-worked machinery to turn out woven goods, felt, and beaver hats, but America knew little of real manufacturing, and fireside industries supplied many articles for market. Households followed their trades at home, wove woolen and linen cloth, knit hosiery, shaped wooden buttons and shoe pegs. A flock of sheep furnished occupation to a whole family. Father and the boys did the shearing, mother and daughters carded, spun, and knitted.

For a hundred years the chief products of the South had been tobacco, rice, and indigo. Cotton was but little raised, due to the fact that a slave picking steadily all day long could separate only a pound of cotton from its seeds, a process so expensive that none but the wealthy could buy cotton. In 1793 Eli Whitney invented a cotton gin that would do the work of fifty slaves at the mere turning of a crank—and so laid the foundation of the great cotton empire of the South. Planters rushed to buy gins that, requiring only two men to operate them, would yield as much as forty pounds of clean cotton per day.

Much of the nation's business was transacted through the trade-and-barter system. The only "hard" money available was foreign coins, very scarce, often chopped into "bits" for change, and, woefully, often counterfeit. In 1792 a law was enacted to establish a mint in Philadelphia. Here was turned out the first American coin money—splendid golden eagles, silver dollars, silver dimes, and copper cents.

The young United States had just cause for pride in its achievements. A census taken in 1790 showed a population of three and a half million. This same year the District of Columbia was established as the site of the seat of government, and the next year the capital city of Washington was laid out. President Washington himself laid the cornerstone of the Capitol building in 1793. Two years later a handsome Executive Mansion was begun.

American Homespun

At the solemn ceremony when he took the oath of office as President of the United States, Washington had proudly worn a suit of American manufacture—coat, waistcoat, and knee breeches of dark brown broadcloth, with white silk stockings, and black shoes with silver buckles.

Years earlier, when England had first passed the harsh laws forbidding her colonies to do any weaving, shoemaking, or hatmaking that might interfere with the prosperity of British manufacturers, the colonials had angrily sung:

> If homespun they say is not quite so gay
> As brocade, yet be not in passion:
>> Just make yourself easy,
>> Let none tax ye or tease ye,
> Make Homespun American fashion.

A patriotic American would wear only "American-made" clothes. To send a boy off to the army suitably equipped, mothers and sisters sat up nights spinning, weaving, sewing. Coat and breeches were made from wool sheared from the family sheep, shirt from home-grown flax, or from cotton laboriously pulled from the seeds by hand.

To oppose the British army of "redcoats" the Continentals adopted a uniform of blue and buff, topped by a cocked hat decorated with a black-and-white cockade. But not every soldier had such a splendid outfit. Leather hunting shirt, fringed leggings, and coonskin cap were good enough for the frontier sharpshooters.

When the Liberty Bell rang out, feminine fashions were

stately and stiff. Bodices were tight, skirts spread out over enormous hoops. A high hair-do was brushed up over cushion pads and sprinkled with powder. Gentlemen whitened their hair with powder too. They had discarded wigs, but dressed their own hair to resemble a wig, puffed it out at the sides, plaited the back hair into a queue or pigtail, and tied it with a black ribbon. Narrow wrist ruffles showed below tight cuffs. Breeches were knee-length, skintight, and buckled at the side of the knee.

The war had been a revolt against a king's tyranny. Now came a revolt against the tyranny of stiff, uncomfortable clothes. First to benefit were the children. For hundreds of years they had been dressed like little men and women. Their running and playing had been hampered by buckram-stiffened coats. Their bodies had been pinched by whalebone stays. Now, at last, they had a style of their own—comfortable round jackets and pantaloons for small boys; soft, loose-hanging frocks for small girls.

Soon the grown-ups were copying the youngsters' comfortable style. Away with hoops and stiff brocades, cried the ladies. Can anything be more charming than soft muslin made into a high-waisted, narrow-skirted gown? Down with the high hair-do. Clip the hair into short curls. At home wear a ruffled mobcap with a bow across the front. Buy a broad-brimmed hat trimmed with ribbons and plumes.

Men got themselves into pantaloons that hung below the knee and were tied with strings instead of fastened with a buckle. They cut their flared coats down to two narrow tails. They laid aside the three-cornered cocked hats that had been high fashion for a hundred years, and bought beaver hats with tall crowns and narrow brims.

American manufacturers set to spinning and weaving. Stout serges, sheer calicoes, and muslins came to market patriotically colored "Congress Brown, Federal Blue, Independence

Green." It was the manufacturers' hard luck, though, that folks no longer bought yards and yards of cloth to make a single garment.

> Alack-a-day, it is the way,
>   Of Fashion's whim and fad,
> To elaborate proportions great
>   When *little*'s to be had.
> But to admire and require,
>   When *much* lies on the shelf,
> The sleeve so tight and skirt so light
>   To slim her stylish self.

Liberty Tea

Patriotism changed American drinking habits. The colonials had enjoyed their imported tea served from a silver teapot on a mahogany table. England's hated tea tax put a stop to this enjoyment. Patriots tarred and feathered un-American tea-swillers, and themselves turned to drinking coffee, or brewed Liberty Tea from the dried leaves of American garden herbs.

From the very beginning of the war army rations were scanty, and they got scantier as defeat followed defeat. The Continental soldier was often thankful to get a handful of corn to parch in the hot ashes of his campfire. Home eating, too, felt the pinch of war. While the men who provided the food were away fighting, a band of enemy soldiers was likely to ride up any day and clear out what hams and sausage were still left hanging in the smokehouse.

Peace brought bounty back to American tables. Low-beamed kitchens with smoke-blackened walls were busy places again. Fires roared in bricked ovens in preparation for bread and cake baking. Fireplace pots, skillets, and bake kettles were called into use, for salting down the meat, preserving the fruit, making strawberry wine and rose-petal cake flavoring, and at least once a week brewing a mild, pleasant beer for the daily beverage. A woman needed four hands. And she also needed information beyond that contained in a reprinted English cookbook whose author had never stirred up maize meal nor roasted wild turkey.

The year 1796 brought the first published cookbook of American authorship. This was titled *American Cookery*, and it featured native foods. Indian corn appeared in breads, batter cakes, muffins, mush. There were puddings of pumpkin and squash; sweet potato dishes, and conserves of berries. Beef, lamb, pork, and chicken were roasted, stewed, baked into pies. Sweets included fruit pies, cake, trifles, whips, puddings, tarts. Measurements were ample, and the cook was instructed to "dry the flour well in the oven, roll the sugar fine, and heat the oven with dry wood."

Many cake recipes called for "emptins", which was some- times hop emptyings saved from the beer brewing, sometimes the lees taken from cider. This ferment swelled the dough in a short time, made it soft and light, though the housewife was advised that "too much of such leaven doth render the bread bitter."

Round Rooms and Eagle-foot Furniture

Proud new United States citizens demanded new-style houses. They were bored with red brick colonial houses and rooms unimaginatively square, so they would add a few round or octagonal rooms for pleasing variety, gaze through an arch into an alcove, ascend circular stairs from a semicircular re- ception hall, put a fanlight over the front door and flank it with sidelights, round off the tops of the windows and cut the openings to floor level and install three instead of two up-and- down-sliding sash so folks could walk right through to bal-

cony or terrace, dignify the front portico with tall white
columns rising two stories in height, and hide the rather flattened hip roof behind an eaves balustrade.

New-style houses required new-style furniture. The popular cabinetmakers, Sheraton and Hepplewhite, offered fragile-
looking little chairs with straight legs and elaborately carved
back panels. Certainly it was not restful to lean against urns,
eagles, and scrolls; but in this day of formal manners no lady
or gentleman would be caught lounging. Writing desks were
elevated on slender legs. Now, for the first time, the dining
room was outfitted with dining table, armchair and side chairs,
and a sideboard to match. The bald eagle had become the
emblem of American patriotism, so up-to-the-minute cabinetmakers set great gilded eagles atop handsome wall mirrors,
carved eagles on chair backs and sofa backs. The popular
eagle-foot sofas stood on eagle claws of brass.

Even as the founding of the American colonies saw pewter
taking the place of wooden tableware, the founding of the
American nation saw china displacing pewter. With true
patriotic ardor the new china dinner sets were decorated with
red-white-and-blue flags, with golden eagles in a frame of stars.
Old people, however, complained of the hardness and slick-
ness of the china plates, saying that the china dulled the knife
when they cut their meat, and that they couldn't anchor the
prongs of the fork firmly as they could in the soft pewter.

Not everyone, of course, could afford the new-style houses
complete with oval salon and classic columns. Many home-
builders contented themselves with arched windows and a
curving staircase. And many, many more built small wooden
houses with never a curve inside or out. Because every board
must be sawed by hand, and every brick shaped by hand labor,
the cost of ornamentation was prohibitive except to the
wealthy. About this time, however, two inventions were patented—the circular saw and a brick-making machine—that

1. Revolutionary period house. 2. Valley Forge. 3. Eagle-foot sofa.
4. Enclosed washstand.

in the fifty years to follow were to put fancy trim on dwellings
within reach of even modest purses.

To the many people moving westward the log cabin in the
backwoods offered only a single room and a wide-mouth
fireplace to house and warm the whole family. But even
pioneers brought with them, over the hard mountain trail, a
precious mahogany table or an eagle-carved chest of drawers.

Prose and Poetry for Patriots

"These are the times that try men's souls. The summer
soldier and the sunshine patriot will, in this crisis, shrink from
the service of their country; but he that stands it *now*, deserves
the love and thanks of man and woman."

So wrote the inspired pen of one Tom Paine. His pamphlets,
Common Sense and *The Crisis*, printed by hundreds and thou-
sands, helped turn men's minds toward independence from
England.

Certain newspapers also fed fuel to the flame of liberty.
From flimsy ink-blurred sheets people read of the signing of
the Declaration of Independence, read reports of the Continental Congress, read of retreats and victories. Wartime
editions, however, appeared somewhat irregularly as both
printer and press often kept just two jumps ahead of an in-
vading army. Peacetime editions then returned to reprints of
foreign news and brief notices of national politics, bumper
crops, marriages and deaths. News, a non-paying item, yielded
front-page importance to advertisements that paid cash. Issues
of April, 1789, even relegated to page two the announcement
of the election of "the Illustrious George Washington, Es-
quire" as first President of the United States, while page one
gave notice of fresh shipments of "Spirits and Sugars from
Jamaica" and "Lemons from Cadiz." But the death of Wash-

ington ten years later brought out mourning editions with columns bordered in black.

American authors were busily dipping quills in inkwells. The first American novel, *The Power of Sympathy or the Triumph of Nature*, was published in 1789. People who read novels were considered light-minded by more solemn persons. But whole families sat together to listen to father read aloud from Mr. Barlow's epic poem, *The Vision of Columbus*, wherein the great Columbus beholds the march of American history from the time of his westward voyaging to independence won. Mr. Trumbull's mock epic, *McFingal*, roused patriotic chortles over the tarring and feathering of "Squire McFingal who had grown, the vilest Tory in the town." But young listeners preferred Mr. Hopkinson's stirring ballad, "The Battle of the Kegs", and its mockery of the English soldiers' alarm over kegs of gunpowder floated downriver to annoy their warships lying at anchor at Philadelphia.

> The cannons roar from shore to shore,
> The small arms make a rattle;
> Since wars began I'm sure no man
> E'er saw so strange a battle.

District School

"Toe the crack," ordered the schoolmaster, "and speak out plain—no humbly-mumbly like a mouse in a cheese." Feet shuffled obediently to line up with the plank flooring, as the advanced class in reading prepared to give its regular morning performance of two verses each from the Bible. This was district school, first fruit of the revolutionary new idea that everyone, even girls, should have a chance at book learning.

War had turned college buildings into barracks. Schools had been closed as master and boys went off to fight. The schools that continued to keep open did so under difficulties, master and pupils fleeing at the approach of an enemy band, coming together again after the danger was past. But out of America's struggle for independence had come a startling new ideal of education: *that a government by the people should provide education for the people*. In 1785 an Act of Congress set aside certain public lands so that "schools and the means of education shall be forever encouraged." Out of this was born the district school, so called because it was designed to serve a district no larger than the distance a child's two legs could carry him from his home to the schoolhouse. Girls sat on one side of the room, boys on the other, and when the master entered in the morning all rose to "make their manners" —the misses to curtsy, the lads to bow. Paid partly by tax rate, and partly by the parents, the master collected a portion of his salary by "boarding round" with the families of his pupils. As there was no compulsion to attend school, people sent their children, or not, as they pleased.

American schools should have American schoolbooks, decided Mr. Noah Webster, so he wrote a spelling book which, because of its blue paper binding, became known as "the Blue-Black Speller". Unlike the colonial primer's gloomy warning, "As runs the glasse, Man's life doth pass," the Blue-Back Speller's "sentences for easy reading" tended toward such homespun advice as, "Never buy a pig in a poke," and "He who lies down with dogs will get up with fleas." Twice a day the scholars stood for spelling class.

Other schoolbooks followed the success of the speller. Webster published *An American Selection of Lessons in Reading and Speaking*. Morse produced his *Geography*. Pike brought out his *Arithmetic*, composed "for the use of citizens of the United States."

Writing had been viewed in the past as a mysterious art

and not many people knew how to handle a pen. But now writing began to be taught in the district school as well as reading and spelling. An old verse lists the necessary equipment:

> Ten things a Penman should have near at Hand:
> Paper, pounce, pen, ink, knife,
> Hone, rule, plummet, wax and sand.

Private boarding schools offered young ladies instruction in "music, dancing, painting, and all the branches of needlework." Boys who aspired to higher education went on from Latin school to college to take a four-year course that was mainly Latin, Greek, philosophy, and theology. Any college with a hundred students and three buildings was looked upon as vastly flourishing.

Before the end of the century an even more revolutionary idea than the district school startled the educational world. In 1795 the University of North Carolina opened its doors to young men students—the first state-supported university.

Yellow Fever

Late in the colonial period the College of Philadelphia and King's College in New York City opened schools of medicine where young men who desired to be doctors could take courses in pharmacy and surgery. But the mothers, who did all the nursing and much of the household physicking, believed in preventive medicine. As soon as the first warm days of spring rolled around, a "treatment" was in order for the younger members of the family. Herbs were pounded and bitters brewed—which was all very fine except for the boy or girl whose nose was being held while a huge dose of sulphur-and-molasses was poured down the throat. Peruvian bark, the bitterest of the bitter but a known cure for the ague shakes, was administered after meals, the powdered bark stirred into milk or syrup.

American doctors marched to war with the army, set up hospitals in barns and farmhouses. There were not enough instruments, not enough medicines. Lacking any opiate to ease the pain, the patient was given a bullet to bite down on while the surgeon with all possible speed probed the wound, sawed off a shattered limb, or sewed up a gaping cut with a big needle and a linen thread that had been dipped in tallow and turpentine. Where men were crowded together in makeshift camps with inadequate provision for sanitation and impure water, epidemics of measles, dysentery, typhus, and typhoid ravaged the troops. Men died on straw pallets, other patients took their places, and the lice and diseases spread from person to person. The doctors did what they could, but more soldiers died of disease than in battle.

Only a decade after the war was past, a new danger to life threatened Americans. This was the yellow-fever plague of 1793. Families fled in panic from the plague-stricken cities; people who could not flee stayed at home and died, or watched their loved ones die of the burning fever and black vomit. No one, not even the doctors, knew how to stop the spread of the disease. Some put their faith in chewing garlic, others sprinkled vinegar about their rooms, or burned tar smudges and hopefully breathed the pungent smoke. Doctors differed in their treatments: applying a poultice to the neck; trying a plunge in cold water; trying a warm vinegar rub; purging with jalap and calomel, and letting blood freely. Guns were fired in the streets to break up the cloud of "swamp miasma" that was believed to carry the disease. But no one bothered to kill mosquitoes, for no one realized that mosquitoes were the real carriers of the plague.

Coach and Four

America's roads were nothing to brag about, but an effort was made to mend them sufficiently to keep the weekly stage wagons plying between the larger cities. Travelers who rode the stage expected to put up with jolting about on a hard wooden bench. Male travelers also expected to have to get out and push if the wagon stuck in a mudhole.

To travel in one's own carriage was, of course, more genteel than crowding into a public stage. A gentleman on a business trip rolled along in his one-horse two-wheeled sulky, riding chair, or chaise. For a family jaunt, the great four-wheeled coach and four horses must be brought out. The coach's exterior magnificence of shining paint and gilt was only exceeded by its interior magnificence of crimson seat cushions, floor carpet, and silk window shades. The ladies were politely handed in, the gentlemen followed; the coachman leaped to his high seat up front, cracked his whip, and they were off. A coach journey was an experience long to remember. A hamper was packed with wine and cold fowl in case tavern fare was not to the master's taste. Smelling salts had to be carried should the bouncing about make the ladies feel sickish. Shovel and ax were a necessity, for one could not go a dozen miles without having to be got out of a dozen mudholes. Shallow rivers had to be forded, deep rivers ferried over on a clumsy pole boat. On dry land again, the horses strained forward. The tavern must be reached before nightfall, for the lantern by the coachman's box was merely a glass-enclosed candle, more a warning of approach than an aid to vision.

Adventurous folk who set their faces toward the free lands of the back country walked or rode horseback through the forest. Or they drifted downriver on a flatboat. For weeks at a time families lived on these floating houses, their cow, pigs, and chickens penned on deck beside the one-room shack. Women cooked and sewed; men fished and kept an eye out for Indians on the river bank, or for sunken logs that could rip the bottom right out of the boat.

Tall ships under full spread of canvas sailed to far-off China to bring back spices and fine silks. Sailing packets moved up and down the Atlantic coast, conveying freight and passengers —from Boston to New York six days, fare five dollars, meals extra; from New York to Charleston in Carolina, ten days, fare twelve dollars, meals also extra.

On the Delaware River appeared an oddity called a steam-boat—the invention of one John Fitch. Propelled by an arrangement of oars powered by a small steam boiler, the steamboat rushed along at a speed of seven miles per hour. But now was the heyday of the Age of Sail and the public refused to take the steamboat seriously.

People laughed at the steamboat, but they gaped at a balloon ascension. At the invitation of President Washington, the famous French balloonist, Blanchard, visited Philadelphia and took the first American air ride.

Party Games and Stage Plays

People enjoyed something new to look at. The election of Washington as first President brought on a gala season of festivities—balls, street processions through arches of flowers, a horse-drawn float representing a full-rigged "ship of state."

Popular dances took on a military flavor with such names as "The Success of the Campaign" and "Clinton's Retreat". Town social circles attended dancing school and learned to step hornpipes, minuets, and cotillions. To a squeaking fiddle, pioneer lads and lassies stamped the old-time rounds and squares so lustily that the cabin floor creaked.

Prim little misses in curls and silk slippers went to evening parties or routs, from five till ten o'clock. Under the soft glow of candles they turned and curtsied in a dance, and played Woo the Widow, Thread the Needle, and Hunt the Whistle. A proper treat for the occasion was nuts, raisins, cakes, and punch.

Boys romped through Whoop-and-Hide, Leapfrog, Hopscotch. They rolled marbles and flew kites. And they played a variety of ball games—Stoolball, Baseball, Cricket, Fives. A little book of verses tells how some of these games were played:

Base-Ball

The Ball once struck off,
Away flies the Boy
To the next destin'd Post,
And then Home with Joy.

Fives

With what great force the little Ball
Rebounds, when struck against the Wall;
See how intent each Gamester stands;
Watch well his Eyes, his Feet, his Hands.

A circus house was built in Philadelphia for the display of feats of horsemanship, ropewalking and fireworks. Visitors marveled at the queer humped shape of two camels brought from the Eastern deserts, and at the enormous size of Old Bet, the first Asiatic elephant to be seen in America.

During the latter years of the colonial period a few wandering troups of actors had given theatrical performances in unused buildings turned into temporary playhouses, but such "play-acting" had been frowned on by sober-minded folks. Now, however, in several cities, there were theaters with "spacious stage, boxes hung in crimson silk, and an orchestra under the direction of a music master seated at the harpsichord." Popular comedies and tragedies were imported from abroad. But America was producing her own plays too, with plots snatched right out of Revolutionary War victories. *Fort Moultrie* showed a grand sea fight in which the enemy was defeated. Another production which had its audience hanging over box rails and shouting in the pit was *The Battle of Bunker Hill*. Here the "hill" was raised by boards extending from the stage to a bench, the backdrop showed burning houses, real fire was "skillfully handled", and windows on the stage were opened to let out the smoke. A rival company might offer Shakespeare's *Romeo and Juliet*, but that could scarcely oppose a Bunker Hill scuffle showing red-coated soldiers rolling downhill.

Patriotic Songs

Yankee-Doodle could sing as well as he could fight. Indeed, he took his national nickname from a song. Back in the days of the French and Indian War the English soldiers sang "Yankee-Doodle" to poke fun at the greenhorn troopers of the colonial army. But it was such a good tune "for fun or fightin', which we all delight in," that it was taken over by the Americans for their own use and sung back at English coat-tails as they fled from the Battle of Lexington.

Now began a time of American music, inspired by American political events and sung in home, street, camp, and political meeting. People sang about the hated tax on tea:

> Not content with the Stamp Act,
> They tax Fish and Sea;
> And America drench with hot water and Tea.
> Derry down, down, hey, derry down.

Victory and peace were celebrated in joyous song. Washington's inaugural tour under "triumphal bowers" produced numerous presidential marches "composed for the occasion."

Theatrical performers introduced music titled "Washington's Counsel Forever, Huzza" and "Washington and Liberty".

Once again "Trebles, Tenors and Basses" organized in singing schools. Music-lovers attended "Consorts of Musick, Vocal and Instrumental." Young ladies tinkled the harpsichord and sweetly sang "The Soldier's Farewell", "Return, O Love", and "I Have a Silent Sorrow".

But when Sons of Liberty met together they lifted their voices in the stirring old tunes, in "Yankee-Doodle", "Chester", and "The American Alphabet".

> A stands for Americans,
>   Who scorn to be slaves.
> B stands for Boston,
>   Where fortitude freedom saves.
> C stands for Congress,
>   To guard our liberty.
> D stands for Defense,
>   Against force and tyranny.
> Stand firmly A and Z.
> We swear forever to be free.

Louisiana Purchase

Chapter 6

HAIL COLUMBIA (1800-1824)

Capital removed from Philadelphia to Washington—
1800
A Military Academy established at West Point—1801
Louisiana bought from the French—1803
The Barbary pirates licked by the American navy—
1804
Florida purchased from Spain—1819
Layfayette the nation's honored guest—1824

AMERICAN CITIZENS, whether city merchants in top hats, tail coats, and tight pantaloons, or pioneers in leather leggings and coonskin caps, loudly demonstrated their pride in their country. The young United States of America was really getting things done. In 1803, at the stroke of a pen and a cash payment of fifteen million dollars, the nation acquired new land to the extent of some six hundred million acres—the great Louisiana Territory purchased from France. Along with this wonderful buy went mastery of the Mississippi River and the port of New Orleans, and also control of the western plains all the way to the Rocky Mountains. The Lewis and Clark expedition, sent to map and explore the northward extent of the new territory, traveled eight thousand miles by canoe, on horseback, and on foot, to the Pacific Ocean and back. They brought back knowledge of Indian tribes, great rivers, mountains, and prairies. They had found a way across the Rocky Mountains. First on the ground, ahead of the English pushing across Canada and the Russians landing in Alaska, they claimed the Oregon territory for the United States.

In 1819 came another flourish of quill pens and the dusting of sand over signatures on a treaty. For the sum of five million dollars, Spain, while still holding California and the Spanish Southwest, ceded to the United States "all territories lying eastward of the Mississippi River, known by the name of East and West Florida."

The years between the treaties had not been quiet years. A flare-up of war with Tripoli ended in American victory and a treaty allowing American vessels to make trade voyages in the Mediterranean Sea unmolested. Then 1812—and a second war with England.

America got off to a bad start in the war. Her land forces were defeated on the Canadian border. The English blockaded Atlantic ports, bombarded Baltimore, burned the new Capitol at Washington. Throughout these dark days Americans were hard at it building ships. Out of coastal havens tall-masted American battle frigates began to slip. They dared desperate sea fights, blockaded the sea at England's very door. Back in America, General Andrew Jackson was moving south with his "long rifles" from Kentucky. He was joined by Tennesseeans, and at New Orleans added Louisiana Creoles in handsome uniforms. He also added a crew of swarthy, hard-fighting Louisiana pirates from their bayou hide-outs. Intrenched in ditches behind cotton bales, this odd mixture of an army faced the greatest English armament ever sent to the New World— sixty ships, ten thousand troops. On January 8, 1815, they faced it and won. The war was ended. America was victorious.

Peace was signed between the two great English-speaking nations; a peace agreement was also made between the United States and Canada, that there should be no warships on the Great Lakes and the land boundary should not have fortress, soldier, or gun.

President Monroe, in 1822, recognized the independence of the South and Central American republics that had recently revolted from the misrule of Spain. In December, 1823, he went a step further and announced the "Monroe Doctrine" as a safeguard against any future colonization by foreign powers on the two American continents. The United States, he declared, would consider any such attempt a threat to its own peace and safety.

Plain talk: just an unvarnished announcement to the world in general, and to Europe in particular, that Americans wanted to be let alone to develop their own destiny. An important feature in this development was the driving speed of American expansion westward. Men packed up household goods, fruit tree seedlings, the Bible and their families, and started out. Some of them floated down rivers; more of them cut trails and roads. The Three-Notch-Way, straight across the Gulf states, became the Federal Road. The Natchez Trace led down from Tennessee to Natchez on the Mississippi. The Cumberland Road through Maryland to the Ohio and beyond made history as the National Road—main route of westward-faring wagons.

Even before the war with England, America had begun turning territories into states. Ohio became a state in 1803;

Louisiana, 1812; Indiana, 1816; Mississippi, 1817; Illinois, 1818; Alabama, 1819; Maine, 1820; Missouri, 1821. Indian tribes were pushed deeper into forest and swamp. Space was cleared for more white settlers, more cabins with log walls and oiled-paper windowpanes, spinning wheels, hand looms, plowed land, and cattle.

The bulk of the American people lived in villages or in the country. On the great cotton and rice and sugar plantations a gracious mode of life flowered amid fine silver and solid mahogany. Here was the big house, with slave cabins set some distance off. Here was careful planning to make the land feed and clothe every worker on those spreading acres. Business was done through a factor or merchant in town, who sold raw produce and filled orders for silks and wines, for books and musical instruments. Accounts were settled once a year. The small farm also raised its own food, spun its thread, wove cloth for garments and bedding, boiled its soap, dipped its candles. Grain was carried to mill in a sack and brought back as meal or flour. And what was desired in the way of bonnets, boots and shoes, crockery, cutlery, tinware and notions, one looked for at the village store.

The cotton gin settled cotton and slavery on the South. New England had a few factories and mills: these were small buildings housing spindles for twisting thread, looms for weaving, also wooden pounders run by horse-power, for felting woolen cloth. But much of the factory work, such as carding wool and cotton, binding broom straw into brooms, and cutting wooden parts for clocks, still had to be done by hand. Whole families—a man, his wife, even small children—worked in the factories.

New York with its ninety-six thousand inhabitants had become the nation's biggest city. Towns and cities made a show of their Roman-domed public buildings, cobble-paved streets, elegant mercantile establishments, and handsome homes with tall-columned porticoes. Ladies in sheer gowns and plumed poke bonnets, and gentlemen in polished boots and pudding cravats, went to church twice on Sunday, danced at the mid-week assembly.

Among families of wealth, marriages were often arranged by parents or guardians. In pioneer districts youths and maidens were freer of choice. People married young, and families were large. The man was master in his house, his wife's property was his to control. Children were expected to obey without question.

The lavish serving of wines and brandies at social gatherings, the potent "grog" procurable at the tavern, only too often led to drunken brawls. A flare-up of hot words, which it was against a gentleman's honor to retract, might end in the fateful words: "Choose your weapons. Meet me beneath the oak at dawn." Pistols for two—another duel—another death.

Dueling was forbidden by law; but hotheads continued to fight duels. The slave trade was made unlawful in 1808, but swift ships continued to slip in and out of harbors—pirate "black-birders" bringing in forbidden human cargoes.

America had inherited the old English common law with its long list of crimes punishable by death. Thoughtful minds, however, were beginning to lean toward imprisonment and work as substitute for the noose, for ear-cropping and branding with a hot iron. Other wrongs needed righting too. Mindful of the wretchedness caused by drunkenness, temperance societies were organized to drive out Old Demon Rum.

A great religious revival swept the country. Fiery preaching stirred men's hearts, brought converts by scores and hundreds to the "sinners' bench". Camp meetings were held under the shelter of "bush arbors". People journeyed long distances by carriage or saddle or on foot, camped in hastily-set-up cabins, enjoyed the companionship, the picnic fare, and singing. Here, at camp meeting, was democracy in the making.

Carriage folks, and those who walked, sat on the same hard bench and lifted voices in the same hymns.

Attending "public speakings" was a national pastime—and especially on the Fourth of July. Independence Day festivities in town opened with a parade of the militia in the morning. At night, marching flambeau clubs performed fiery drills with whale-oil torches on broomsticks. Country folks celebrated with horse races, shooting matches, and a big basket dinner. But, town or country, the crowning glory of the day was the flag-draped stand, the spellbinding orator, and then every-body standing to sing "Hail, Columbia, happy land."

Yankee-Doodle on a Slack Rope

An Exhibition of Rope Dancing. The Performer will execute many extraordinary feats—will appear on the Slack Rope with his Head tied up in a Sack, Fireworks on each arm, and Dancing to the tune of Yankee-Doodle.

Proud citizens seemed never to tire of celebrating their country's victories. Acrobats stunted to the national airs. Theaters featured musical interludes with the audience lustily lifting voice in "The Freedom of the Seas" and "Yankee Tars". Couples swung corners and balanced in line as they danced to the martial strains of "Hull's Victory".

Dancing was popular entertainment the length and breadth of the land. But into the midst of the familiar hornpipes and reels now exploded a startling new dance—the waltz, a "turning-couple dance" imported from Central Europe. Shocked whispers greeted its dizzy whirling and its "im-modest" dancing position. Instead of leading his lady by the fingertips of one hand as in the quadrille, the waltzer drew his partner close in a two-handed grasp. Even worse, he some-times placed a polite and genteel hand on the lady's back as he whirled away with her.

There were card games to suit every sort of player. Mississippi flatboatmen, on their layover in New Orleans, picked up the exciting French game of Three-card Poque, which, under the name of Poker, was presently to develop into a "favorite sport" of American males. Gentlemen indulged in "snug little parties at Brag." A pleasing game for the ladies was Loo, with its excitement of "looing" one's adversary.

Shopkeepers advertised "Dominoes, Backgammon Boards, Chess Men of Ivory," also a "Picture Puzzle" that when put together turned out to be a map of America.

Early in the nineteenth century the circus ceased to be a big city affair presented beneath the roof of a circus house. Rolling shows took to the road. They were small—just a couple of horse-drawn wagons and a half-dozen performers. In place of a tent, a canvas wall high enough so none could peek over it was stretched around sharpened stakes driven into the ground. There were no seats; everybody just stood and thrilled to the sight of tumblers and pole-vaulters, jig-dancers and funny-faced clowns.

Steamboats and Stagecoaches

Another wonderful sight was a steamboat plowing upstream with engines roaring, black smoke pouring from tall stacks, sparks flying, and great paddle wheels throwing spray high in the air. Jealous captains of rival sailing sloops darkly prophesied that people who rode these "swimming volcanoes" would be blown to bits or burned to a cinder.

Previous to that August day in 1807 when Fulton's *Clermont* chugged up the Hudson under the power of steam, the forces that moved America's river boats had been brawny arms poling a flatboat or wind in spread of canvas. But the idea of steam power quickly caught on. By 1814 three paddle-

1. Lewis and Clark expedition. 2. *Old Ironsides.* 3. "The Star-Spangled Banner." 4. "Fulton's Folly," the *Clermont.*

wheelers were splashing up and down the Mississippi at the speed of four miles per hour upstream, ten down.

These amazing new craft were called "steamboats", but rightly they were steamships, for they were as pointed of bow and narrow of hull as any deep-sea sailing ship. It remained for Henry Shreve, a Mississippi keelboatman, to design and build the first real steamboat, the *President Washington*, in 1816. Instead of a ship's hull, weighted down with machinery till it dragged on every sandbar, Shreve used a flatboat-type hull, one that would float on the water instead of in the water. He placed his machinery on deck instead of in the hold, and added an upper deck containing a dining salon surrounded by staterooms and a railed promenade where passengers could take the air.

The sailing ship was still mistress of the ocean. In 1816 the Black Ball Line established a regular transatlantic service with liners scheduled to sail for certain ports on certain days. This was a wonderful convenience for people who grew weary of waiting while a cargo vessel picked up a load. Now passengers could cross the ocean in thirty days by fast packet sloop; in forty days if seas ran high.

The first steamship to try the ocean crossing was the *Savannah*, which in May, 1819, steamed out of Savannah, Georgia, bound for England. Insufficient fuel necessitated going most of the way under sail, but enough coal was hoarded to be able to steam into Liverpool harbor after twenty-nine days at sea. Because of the difficulty of carrying enough coal or firewood to make such long voyaging profitable, the *Savannah* was stripped of engine and paddle wheels and ended her days as a sailing vessel.

Increased land travel demanded better roads, so private companies began building turnpikes or smoothly graveled roadways barred every few miles by turngates where travelers paid toll for the privilege of riding on the pike. Over the turnpike rumbled trains of freight wagons. A private coach rolled swiftly along, the driver perched up front, the ladies within swaying comfortably upon curved iron springs. As regular as the clock came the stagecoaches, painted a splendid blue, yellow, or green. Carriages and wagon trains turned aside to let the galloping horses and the great rocking coaches dash past.

Now was the heyday of coaching. The jolting stage wagon with hard board benches and sides open to wind and rain had evolved into the huge, round-bottomed stagecoach, with driver on box, cushioned seats within, and glass in doors and windows. Places were provided for nine passengers—six inside, one up beside the driver, two at the back sitting high up over the boot or luggage compartment. A horn blast announced arrival and departure. The finest stages averaged six to eight miles per hour on the turnpike.

Relay stations dotted the turnpike every ten miles: here it was snapping-off of harness and buckling-in of a fresh four-horse team every four minutes. Gentlemen in high silk hats, usually the soul of courtesy, hustled wives in narrow skirts up the coach steps with scant grace. Bonnet boxes were tumbled in. With crack of whip, leap of horses, they were off at top speed in all the horn-blowing, passenger-shouting excitement of a race with a rival coach.

The Male Academy with a Female Department

In this hustling, bustling America not everyone could afford to go to college, yet there were many ambitious young people who wanted more learning than just "the Three R's" obtained at district school. Taxpayers, however, couldn't be expected to provide everything free. The answer was the private academy that accommodated day and boarding pupils. By providing three departments—classical, English, and female

—the academy offered girls as well as boys a chance at higher education. The Latin and Greek courses prepared young men for college. In the English department rhetoric was a featured study, for in this gloriously free country any boy might be called to a seat in the legislature via the course in "Rhetoric and Public Speaking." The female department was discreetly separate from the male. In town or village the academy was a dominant structure, usually a large red brick building topped by a cupola and bell. The day began early, and rules of behavior were strict. Charges, however, were not unreasonable: "Tuition $8 to $15; Board, Washing and Lodging at $45 per annum."

The one-room district school had now become "the little red schoolhouse"—red paint being the cheapest money could buy. Town schools kept six days a week eleven months a year. Country schools divided the year into two terms. The summer term, from May till August, was for small children and was under a schoolmistress. Winter term, from Thanksgiving to March, was for the big boys and girls who were needed on the farm during planting and harvest. This was taught by a master who believed in "lickin' and larnin' ". Lessons were "blabbed" in loud whispers to the accompaniment of squeaking slate pencils. There were no classes except in reading and spelling. Each pupil memorized his grammar rules, worked his sums, or wrote his lines in a copybook, then marched up to the master's desk, recited what he had learned, and was set a new stint. In the weekly spelling match both boys and girls strove for the honor of spelling down all rivals.

America could now boast twenty-four colleges with a total enrollment of some two thousand young men. A typical college course, the one and same for all students, began and ended in Latin and Greek, with some theology, law and science in between. A bell, known as "the Sacred Rouser," called to morning prayers by candlelight. Study and recitations occupied the day. Evenings were given over to literary meetings and the debating society.

State universities were multiplying. Georgia, South Carolina, Ohio, and Maryland opened their doors early in the century. Virginia, in 1819, despite outraged cries of "godlessness", chartered its university minus a theological department, and thus set the style for future free and secular state-supported schools.

The Library Society

Nearly every city had its library society, which was a gentlemanly association for the enjoyment of good reading. Some societies were newly founded, others traced back to colonial days, but all provided quiet reading rooms, a table with magazines and newspapers, chairs, and candlelight. Bookshelves were filled with the Greek and Roman classics, theology, law, biography, history, arts, and sciences, with a sprinkling of novels, tales, and poetry—just what one would expect to find in a gentleman's private library. Members paid dues and were privileged to borrow books for themselves and their families.

There were no library societies in the back country. Occasionally, though, when a wagon train made a trip to town, a bundle of skins would be sent along to exchange for books. The volumes in those "buckskin libraries" would be passed from hand to hand till read to tatters.

People who kept up with the newest books had a choice of three *Lives* of Washington. They laughed over Mr. Irving's tongue-in-cheek *Knickerbocker's History of New York*, and they simply couldn't put down Mr. Tyler's exciting novel *The Algerine Captive, a Tale of Piracy and Adventure*.

Young readers were dosed on "improving tales", as *Waste Not, Want Not; or Two Strings to Your Bow*, and *Caution-*

ary Stories in Verse. It was more fun to read "Twinkle, Twinkle, Little Star", and then look for a star to wish on. But the
most fun of all was to open "A Visit from St. Nicholas", published in 1823, and read aloud to an eager circle of small
brothers and sisters, " 'Twas the night before Christmas . . ."
and on and on about Dancer and Prancer and Jolly Saint Nick.

Roman Domes and Arches

The books people read had a visible effect on the houses
they built. In the Latin classics they read that mighty Rome,
like their own young United States, had once been a fledgling
republic. They saw it as fitting, therefore, that Roman architecture should be the one style worthy of soaring American
ambition. Truly, it seemed almost unpatriotic to erect a public building and not front it with a Roman portico and top it
with a Roman dome. Many a Latin-reading, English-speaking
pioneer in his one-room log cabin dreamed of the splendidly
porticoed mansion he would someday build.

Roman-style houses were quite different from anything
colonial carpenters and bricklayers had put up for father and
grandfather to dwell in. Instead of being "homey", the new
houses were impressive. Massive round arches supported a
white-columned portico at second-story level. Handsome stone
steps led up to the portico, to upstairs parlor and back parlor.
It was considered wise to have the sleeping rooms high also,
and thus above reach of the creeping, fever-laden swamp
miasmas.

In contrast to the bold design of the exterior, interior decorations suggested fragile elegance. Spiral stairs curved upward
without visible support. Walls were tinted in delicate colors,
or papered with expensive scenic wallpaper imported from
France. Woodwork was painted white. Golden yellow damask

or rose taffeta formed valances and festoons over the tall, narrow windows. Parlor floors were softened by flowered carpets. A mirror in a gilded frame hung above a white marble mantel.

Frail-looking French-style furniture was ornamented with inlay instead of carving. Satin-upholstered sofas and lyre-back chairs—the back panel cut in the shape of the classic harp or lyre—stood on spindly legs curving outward. Another musical whimsey was the lyre-pedestal drum table with top like a drum. A choice item for the dressing room was a cheval glass or tall standing mirror lighted by candles supported on hinged arms. A French importation was the Napoleon or sleigh bed made with outward curving headboard and footboard. But a purely American innovation was the banjo clock to hang on the wall. Much in demand was furniture designed by Duncan Phyfe, the famous American cabinetmaker.

Guests to dinner sat in lyre-back or fiddleback chairs at a twin-pedestal table and ate off bone-white china decorated with a gold wreath. Or, if the hostess preferred, she could set her table with a complete dinner service of cut glass—"plates, covered dishes, cake and sweetmeat dishes, sugar bowl, goblets, cups and saucers, and also a large punch bowl."

Empire Gowns and Pudding Cravats

French fashions in dress were à la mode. From the France of Emperor Napoleon came milady's Empire gown—a narrow-cut, short-waisted, one-piece dress that fell softly to the feet. Necklines were very high or very low—either a choker collar with chin-tickling ruffle, or the bosom almost bare. Colors were delicate and materials gauzy. Not to spoil the gown's clinging lines, the chemise and petticoat must be of equal thinness and scanty cut. For warmth one put on a spencer (a short jacket) or a pelisse (a long coat). White silk stockings

were worn with heelless slippers of silk or kid. Hair was
dressed in loose ringlets and a twisted knot. There were ruffled
muslin mobcaps for home wear, lace caps for evening parties.
Young ladies sported broad-brimmed gypsy hats of straw.
Ladies young and old decked themselves in scoop-brim poke
bonnets lined with silk and adorned with ostrich plumes.

A by-product of the fad for thin materials was the reticule
or handbag of netted silk. Skirts too gauzy to support a pocket
necessitated some outside assistance to hold a lady's handker-
chief, small money, and essence bottle.

The high-waisted soft-flowing Empire styles were wonder-
fully becoming to little girls. In white or pale-colored muslin,
with a silk sash tied under the arms, white stockings, black
kid slippers, a necklace of gold beads, and her hair in short
curls, little miss was a picture to look at. Small boys strutted
in ankle-length pantaloons, short jacket, and a stovepipe hat
"like Papa's."

Among American males the Battle of Breeches was raging
furiously. The seventeenth and eighteenth centuries had been
the Era of Knee Breeches; the nineteenth century was to become the Era of Pantaloons—but not before masculine leg
wear had become a badge of political conviction. Conserva-
tive-minded gentlemen arranged their long hair in powdered
queues and stepped sedately in knee breeches and silver buckles. Men of more modern outlook cut their hair short, put on
skin-tight pantaloons and top boots. Coats were short-waisted
and long-tailed. Shirts were ornamented down front with a
pleated frill. A black silk tie was knotted in a bow over a stiff
standing collar, or a pudding cravat of starched white linen
was wound around the neck right up to the ears.

> " 'A Man of Fashion, sir,' he proudly said.
> 'My cravat's so stylish I can't turn my head.' "

An Operation without Anesthesia

Doctors were concerned over the fashion for thin muslin gowns and thin silk cloaks. They issued grave warnings that if females didn't dress more warmly they'd all die of the consumption. Rheumatism was the crippler of the aged, but consumption or lung disease struck at the young. Maidens were prone to "fall into a decline" that racked frail bodies with coughing and splotched thin cheeks with the bright red of hectic fever.

With the United States steadily spreading southward and westward, and with its population increasing by leaps and bounds, there were not enough doctors to go around. A medico often rode miles on horseback to answer a call. If necessary, he sat up all night with a patient. And he did a little dentistry as a side line, charging twenty-five cents per tooth pulled; two or more at a reduced price. Fees commonly ran: one dollar a visit, twelve cents a dose, two dollars for a blood-letting. A cupping, which was a favored remedy and consisted of applying a heated cupping glass to draw blood to the surface of the flesh, cost all of four dollars. Lacking a soothing antiseptic, but well aware that something was needed to check infection in a wound, the doctor used hot grease—goose grease or tallow melted to a simmering point and poured right into the festering spot. This was treatment that brought yells of pain, but it could heal a sore in a day or two. For the "dry belly-ache", that terrible pain across the stomach that not infrequently ended in death, he could do nothing. It seemed beyond reach of his most powerful doses.

Where the doctor went, there went quinine. With quinine he could relieve an attack of malarial fever; but he could not stop new cases from breeding. The best he could do was to urge people to act upon the advice given in his medical books:

"Malaria is brought on by breathing swamp miasma. Persons residing in a house where malaria prevails around, should repose at the top of the dwelling, and restrain themselves from leaving home at night or at early dawn."

The dread epidemics came and went, leaving desolation in their wake. To measles, typhus, typhoid, to diphtheria, that killer of children, to the yellow fever "that lurks unseen in the pestiferous atmosphere," one bowed the head. Only with smallpox had a preventive been found. In England the great Dr. Jenner, by 1798, had successfully vaccinated humans with cowpox serum and rendered them immune to smallpox. In 1800 vaccination was brought to America, and enthusiastic doctors began vaccinating everyone they could lay hands on who was not already pock-marked. The professional inoculators who were making money holding "smallpox parties" where people were given mild made-to-order cases as protection against a more deadly attack raised an instant outcry against vaccination. Wild yarns were spread about that children treated with the cowpox serum "grew horns and hoofs and went around bellowing like bulls."

Surgery, in general, was limited to bone-setting, blood-letting, and amputation. To "open the human body to the infected air" was practically to invite the horrors of blood poisoning. Even so, some internal operations were attempted. A long table was covered with a sheet; a smaller table held basin of warm water, knives, needles, silver suture wire, and waxed thread. The patient was strapped to the table and four men took firm hold of wrists and ankles. Few patients survived such an ordeal.

Record, however, is preserved of one operation with a happy ending. On Christmas Day, 1809, Dr. Ephraim McDowell of Kentucky removed a large ovarian tumor from a woman, who, for thirty minutes of agony, received many extra years of life. The success of this operation marked the beginning of abdominal surgery in the United States.

Sauces

> He setteth forth the very best,
>   Of brandy, rum and whiskey,
> Wine and gin and bitter sling,
>   To make his guests feel frisky.

Hospitality demanded that guests be offered liquid refreshments, whether the firewater of the frontier cabin, or the sponge cake and wine, seed cake and punch, of the mansion.

Well-to-do families observed the stylish dinner hour of four o'clock in the afternoon, served rich pastries and wines, meat and fish courses. Sauces to fit such foods were elegant in the extreme—oyster sauce for boiled poultry, mushroom sauce for beefsteak, peach sauce for the roast, caper sauce for the mutton, and at the end of the meal a sweet sauce for the pudding.

A visitor to New Orleans, where generations of French settlers had made cookery a fine art, found more sauces to tickle his palate—saffron sauce with turtle, little sausages sauced with pimiento. He also found a pleasantly pungent red sauce made from tomatoes. Very probably, though, he viewed this sauce with suspicion, for many folks feared the "poisonous love apple", as the tomato was called.

If the stranger happened to go into one of New Orleans' famous eating places, his first course might be meat soup, followed by a casserole of meat and vegetables. Just as he laid down his two-tined fork and broad-bladed knife and prepared to depart, the rest of the courses came: fricasseed chicken, fish fried in olive oil, lamb kidneys in wine, a dessert of almond paste and fruits, sherry with brandy. Finally, coffee, and a little pan of glowing coals for lighting up his pipe.

Singing the Shapes

New Orleans had its French opera where ladies in embroidered mull, and gentlemen in high cravats, crowded the boxes to cry "Viva!" and hurl bouquets at the feet of their favorite sopranos and tenors. In less sophisticated areas of the U.S.A. people were "singing the shapes." In a burst of patriotism numerous rural singing-school teachers discarded British-printed music books and compiled their own tune books. *The American Harmony, The Delights of Harmony,* and various song books were rushed through the presses. To simplify musical matters the modern scale of seven tones was also thrown into the discard, and the ancient four-syllable scale was revived. To help people learn to read music faster, this four-scale sequence was marked by notes of different shapes—as triangle, round, square, diamond—and one could tell at a glance just what each note was.

"Now, all together." The singing master beat time in long, rhythmic strokes. "Fa sol la mi," chanted his pupils. At singing school it was customary to sing the shapes till a tune was familiar, then progress to singing the words. A group trained to sing the shapes needed no instrument to help their harmonies. Singing masters moved westward and southward, carrying a knowledge of music in general and the shapes in particular to music-starved pioneer districts. Pupils nailed up rough benches, brought their own candles, and settled down happily to acquiring book singing. Hymn tunes and ballads vied for favor. Especially suitable for the last song of a singing session was "The Parting Hand":

> O could I stay with friends so kind,
> How it would cheer my drooping mind;
> But duty makes me understand
> That we must take the parting hand.

While the "shapes" were intrenching themselves in the back country, city dwellers held to more polished music. New-style pianofortes were replacing outmoded spinets and harpsichords; but the handsomest addition to an elegant drawing room was a great golden harp. Ladies adored the harp, knowing full well how charming they looked as they sat with white arms uplifted to the strings. The harp's rippling runs were the perfect accompaniment to a sweet voice singing:

> "I'll watch for thee from my lonely bow'r,
> Come o'er the sea at the twilight hour."

Out of the war with Britain sprang a song written in one dawning and made famous before the dawning of another day. On the night of September 13, 1814, Francis Scott Key of Baltimore was held prisoner aboard a British battleship in the harbor. All night he watched the bombardment of his native city. In the dawn, thrilling to the sight of the American flag still flying above the fort, he scribbled some verses on a scrap of paper. That night, an actor, serving with the American troops, stood before a crowd of people and sang:

> "The star-spangled banner in triumph shall wave,
> O'er the land of the free and the home of the brave."

Chapter 7

HUSTLE AND BUSTLE (1825-49)

Boats pulled by horses on the Erie Canal—1825
Railway cars pulled by a steam locomotive in Carolina
  —1831
Cyrus McCormick's reaping machine invented—1831
S. F. Morse's electric telegraph patented—1837
Elias Howe's sewing machine patented—1845
A Women's Rights Convention—1848
Gold found in California—1849

THE GIRL in shoulder puffs and embroidered pantalets, and
the boy in roundabout and pantaloons, stared at the man in
the tall beaver hat as he lighted his pipe with a flame he'd
struck from a tiny stick he took out of his pocket. "Pfeu! It
stinks!" The boy made a face.

With wonderful inventions popping up practically every
day this was an exciting time in which to be living. Those

friction matches, or lucifers, as they were named, smelled vilely of sulphur fumes but were quick to blaze when struck on a bit of sandpaper. From fields all over the country sounded the whirr of horse-drawn reaping machines that could cut a stand of wheat faster than ten men. Then there was a contraption of wheels and rods and a needle, called a sewing machine, which sailmakers were using to stitch up their yards and yards of canvas for sailing ships. Women, stitching up their family's clothes by hand, were talking pretty enviously about this sewing machine. Up-to-the-minute cities, instead of hanging out a lantern on a pole, were making their streets as bright as day with gas lamps lit each evening by a lamplighter who hurried from lamppost to lamppost to touch off the blazing gas jet. But it was the railroads that were causing the biggest stir. "Egad, sir. Even if a way to fly should be invented, who'd endure the nuisance of wearing a pair of wings and the labor of flapping them, when every gentleman may keep his own locomotive and travel from the Mississippi to the Atlantic with no other expense than a teakettle of water and a basket of chips?"

Yes, it was a hustling, bustling time. Things were happening everywhere. In 1822 Mexico had won her independence from Spain; and Texas, New Mexico, and California became part of the Mexican republic. Immediately Missouri wagon trains had started hauling freight across the seven hundred miles of rolling plains to Santa Fe. American colonists began swarming down into the province of Texas where lands were apparently limitless and certainly fertile. The Mexican authorities became alarmed, forbade further immigration, and enacted oppressive laws. Promptly the Texans rose in revolt, and in 1836 declared themselves the independent Republic of Texas. But Texans had to fight for their freedom. Out of bitter defeat came the battle cry, "Remember the Alamo!" that spurred them on to victory at San Jacinto and independence.

Up through the northwest wilderness went pioneers in canvas-covered wagons guided by fur trappers. They ventured through dim canyons, climbed towering heights, to at last look down into the great valley of the Columbia. The Oregon Trail had been opened. The conquest of Oregon had begun.

An upsurge toward democracy or government by the people, as opposed to government by the high-born and rich, swept the nation. With vim and gusto, bricklayers and stevedores and farmers and thousands of other men who worked with their hands voted General Andrew Jackson, the hero of the Battle of New Orleans, into the Presidency.

Two new states were added, Arkansas in 1836, Michigan in 1837. The 1840 census-takers reported a population of seventeen million. Two burning political questions were on everyone's tongues. What to do about Texas? What to do about Oregon? The annexation of the Republic of Texas, and the making of it into an American state, brought on war with Mexico. Out of this struggle came undisputed possession of Texas, and also the addition of California and New Mexico to the United States. While the cannon were still booming on the Mexican border, America was making bold talk that could lead to war with England over the Oregon border. Settlers in the northwest were demanding: "The whole of Oregon or none! Fifty-four Forty or Fight!" America didn't get the 54° 40′ boundary line. And England didn't fight. The land was divided by treaty, America's part to begin at the forty-ninth parallel and to contain some two hundred and fifty thousand square miles.

Cotton was king in the South where thousands of black slaves tended the ever-spreading fields. Many of the slaves were well cared for, others suffered under brutal masters or overseers. But for good or ill the plantation system was built upon slave labor. Now was the magnificent peak of Southern plantation life. More cotton planted, more cotton baled and sold, meant more money to spend on elegant silks, furniture, crystal, and silver. Tutors and governesses were engaged for the small children, daughters were trained in the social accomplishments. Occasionally a son would make the grand tour of Europe to complete his education. From the white-columned Greek temple mansion, where there was abundance of food, rooms, servants, flowed a gracious hospitality.

The North was turning to industry. On every watercourse could be heard the clang of machinery spinning and weaving cotton into cloth, shaping clay into china plates, cutting brass and steel into knives, clockworks, and a thousand useful things. Towns sprang up around the factories. Dominating the dwellings of the factory workers, the streets of shops and stores, even the church spire and the cupola on the college built by wealth flowing out from the factory, was the big house on the hill—the home of the factory owner.

Among comfortably well-to-do families a new pattern of life was showing. Papa still worked hard at his counting house, office or store, but mamma and daughters, now that many household necessities were factory-made and store-bought, had more leisure time for visiting, reading, doing their fancy needlework. They also had time to march and sing in temperance rallies. They even dared think about trying to change certain man-made laws so as to better the condition of working women and children. By 1848 they were meeting in a women's rights convention.

In sober truth, working women needed some "rights". With the invention of power machinery the old-time hearthside industries had moved into the factory—and had taken the family with them. Men and women swapped long hours of farm and household work for long hours of factory work. Children labored from daybreak till sundown to add their pennies to the family earnings. Especially bleak was the lot of the wage-earning female. Top pay for a man was seventy cents a day, and she got less. And worse, if she were married, her husband could legally take her pay, and, if he so desired, spend it on grog for himself instead of on food and clothing for the family.

Religious feeling expressed itself in a variety of ways. Children were shined up and sent to Sunday school. Families sat together in their pews through morning and afternoon sermons. Camp-meeting preaching drew its crowds. Certain persons believed that the end of the world was at hand and set a date in October, 1844.

But the "wicked old world", particularly that part known as the U.S.A., continued on its way in undiminished vigor. Four new stars were added to the flag—Texas and Florida in 1845, Iowa in 1846, Wisconsin in 1848. Runaway slaves from the South made their way to freedom in the North through the helping hands of the Underground Railway.

Then, in 1849, sounded the cry, "Gold in California!"—and the "Forty-Niners" were off in a rush to the west. Men boarded fast clipper ships in New York harbor and headed round Cape Horn, a sixteen-thousand-mile route to the California gold fields. Other men creaked their way over the western plains in prairie schooners, camping in the circle of their covered wagons, twanging banjos, fighting off Indians. In less than a year more than a hundred thousand people had swarmed into California. The settlement of Sacramento mushroomed from twenty-five inhabitants to ten thousand. San Francisco leaped to twenty thousand population in a helter-skelter of plank houses, tent houses, stores, and saloons. At the mining camps, guns and ropes were the only law.

1. Best Friend—engine of Charleston and Hamburg Railroad. 2. Mc-Cormick's reaper. 3. Howe's sewing machine. 4. Gold in California!

Sleeve Puffs and Pantalets

Americans were accomplishing big things, but one would never guess it to look at their clothes. A stylishly gotten up gentleman in wasp-waist coat and curled side whiskers did not look ready to conquer a wilderness. And who would expect a lady in starched petticoats and sleeve puffs to undertake a thousand-mile journey in a covered wagon and handle a gun beside her man in an Indian attack?

Fashion had decreed a change from thin, clinging gowns to frocks of extravagant fullness. Into the discard went pale pink muslins. Out were brought taffeta and plumes, velvet in wine red and royal blue. Sleeve cushions stuffed with feathers puffed out the sleeves at the shoulder to make a lady appear as wide as she was tall. The full skirt was shortened to permit a glimpse of trim ankles. Bodices fitted snugly, waistlines marked by a neat belt. Hair was parted in the middle and brushed smooth over the ears, or arranged in ringlets. Ruffled house caps were popular, though maidens were warned that "no unmarried lady should wear a morning-cap; it is the mark of the young matron." Broad-brimmed hats and bonnets with flaring brims were faced with silk and piled with ribbon bows, plumes, and flowers. Stylish wraps were the paletot or loose coat, the pelerine or shoulder cape, and the tight-fitting polka jacket.

White muslin pantalets, tucked, ruffled, or lace-trimmed, showed beneath the skirt of every stylish miss. Her frock was as puffed of sleeve and wide of skirt as her mamma's. A bibbed apron protected her dress at home and at school.

Men's pantaloons, also called trousers, were long, with a strap passing under the shoe. Pearl gray, plaid, or striped pantaloons were often worn with a green or blue coat. The tail coat was still seen, but the frock coat, with padded shoulders, nipped-in waist, and full skirt reaching to the knees, was crowding it out of favor. A fine linen shirt frill showed above a sprigged silk or velvet waistcoat fastened with glass buttons. A white muslin stock wound around a stiff linen collar was completed by a dark silk cravat tied in a bow. Tall beaver or silk hats bore such names as "chimney-pot", "bell-crowned", "plug" hat.

Boys wore long pantaloons, striped and checked like their papa's, short "roundabout" jackets, and top hats.

Textile mills were taking spinning and weaving out of the home, but the family sewing was still the housewife's job. To make a fine frilled shirt meant endless small stitches and needle-pricked fingers. Men's suits were generally cut and seamed by the local tailor. In 1834 a wholesale manufacture of ready-made suits was begun in New York City. The goods were cut, matched with buttons, thread, and lining, then given out to be made up. Females took home pantaloons, coats, and vests to sew them.

In 1845 Mr. Howe patented his sewing machine. The swiftly flashing needle could run up a seam in the twinkling of an eye but only sailmakers stitching their hundreds of yards to rig fast sailing clippers got any use of the new invention. Tailors and home seamstresses continued to seam and tuck by hand.

Canal Packets and Iron Horses

Not wind in the sails but horses walking a towpath on the canal bank moved the canalboats. Numerous short canals had been dug to connect waterways, but the Erie, completed in 1825, was 363 miles long and stretched across New York State from Lake Erie to the Hudson River. Travel by canal-boat was safe but slow. Canal packets, painted white, and with neat green blinds at tiny windows, did their three to four miles every hour. Within were a ladies' cabin, and a main cabin which served as dining room and also as sleeping room for men and boys, table boards being laid on trestles for each meal, and bunks set up against the wall at night. Travelers got a thrill out of passing through the big stone locks that made it possible for a boat to go up or down hill. The huge wooden doors of the lock swung open, the boat slipped inside, the doors swung shut, and the boat slowly started rising or falling as the water was allowed to rush in or rush out. Then the floodgates opened again and the boat glided out at the desired higher or lower level. If a bridge spanned the canal, someone was sure to sing out a warning to passengers sunning themselves on the roof:

> "Low-bridge yonder, duck your head down!
> Low-bridge bump your head going through town."

Steamboats were splashing up and down rivers. Instead of swimming volcanoes they had become floating palaces with gilt-framed mirrors, lavish spread of fine foods, and fares so cheap as to make travelers disregard the ever-present danger of a boiler explosion. The stern-wheelers, with one huge paddle wheel to push the boat along, were of enormous size— three hundred to four hundred feet in length. Twin smoke-stacks rose above gleaming white woodwork. The lower deck was given over to freight. To the saloon deck and promenade deck were reserved the plush and mahogany elegance of the ladies' cabin, the social hall, the dining saloon.

A trip by canalboat or steamboat often called for a trip by stagecoach to complete the journey. But the stagecoach flashing down the turnpike at six miles an hour, or creaking over stump-cluttered trails (three weeks from the Atlantic to the Mississippi), was already facing a rival in the iron horse on the railroad.

In January, 1831, the locomotive The Best Friend pulled a brigade of cars at twenty-one miles per hour on the Charleston and Hamburg Railroad in South Carolina, the first railroad built for the exclusive use of steam power. Previously there had been a few miles of iron track on which horses pulled the cars. But now the cry was for iron horses, and for more miles of track. Within a decade twenty-three miles of railroad had been stretched to twenty-three hundred miles.

People crowded around to get a look at the splendid locomotive, all of twelve feet long and puffing clouds of smoke from lofty smokestack. Hitched on behind was the tender, loaded with firewood and water barrels. Last came the cars, round-bottomed like stagecoaches. The Master of the Cars blew a blast on a horn. Gentlemen in high silk hats hastily helped ladies in mantelets to their seats. The engineer crammed fat pine into the already red-hot firebox. The train gave a clank and a jerk, and they were off.

Only a hero could run those early steam trains, and only heroes and heroines dared ride them. There was no cowcatcher, no bell, no cab. The engineer stood out in the open and took sun or rain as he dashed onward at the dizzying speed of twenty miles an hour. There was no headlight. If a train had to run at night (which was seldom), a flatcar carrying a pine-knot fire blazing in a sandbox was pushed along in front. The cars had no brakes and at every stop they bumped viciously. Ladies were placed in the rear cars away from flying sparks and a possible explosion. But no seat was entirely safe, for the track was made of wood with a thin iron rail nailed on, and occasionally a rail worked loose, poked up into a car, and speared some luckless passenger. Progress, however, was on the march. Soon iron T-rails were laid. A large whale-oil lamp was fastened on the nose of the locomotive. And a sleeping car, a flat-bottomed box-type car with four sets of three bunks built against one wall, made its appearance in 1836.

On the ocean the new American clipper ships, with their towering canvas and sharp lines, were breaking all speed rec-

ords. A run from China to New York was made in 74 days,
14 hours. Sailing packets followed a fortnightly schedule from
New York to Liverpool, taking about 21 days for the crossing
if the weather were favorable. People thought this remarkably
fast till that day in April, 1838, when the British-built steamship *Sirius*, 16½ days out of Ireland and carrying 94 passengers, dropped anchor in New York harbor. Next morning
another British ship, the *Great Western*, steamed in. America
went wild with excitement.

At Home in a Greek Temple

Romantic Americans were fond of mixing their architecture
with their politics. In the early days of their young republic
they had copied the arches and domes of the ancient Republic
of Rome. Now, with General Andy Jackson in the President's
mansion and democratic ideals to the fore, they suddenly remembered that peerless Athens, the queen city of ancient
Greece, had been a democracy. Instantly, and enthusiastically,
they began building Greek-style houses—but not the plain,
squarish houses the ancient Greeks had lived in. No, proud
young America modeled its dwellings after the colonnaded
temple the Greeks had worshiped in. Folks felt at liberty,
though, to change things around. Some home-builders discarded the gabled roof carrying through from front to rear
and put on a nearly flat roof screened by a balustrade. Others
added wings. But all kept the tall white columns across the
front. Rooms were large and square, with white plastered
walls. Kitchens were set a hundred paces off in the yard.

The taste now was for furniture more sturdy in appearance
than the spindly-legged pieces so much admired earlier in the
century. High-backed rosewood chairs, and sofas with rolled
ends and massive, out-curving supports, were upholstered in

black haircloth. Parlor tables displayed a round marble top raised on a central pillar.

Candles in crystal-drop candelabra or pedestaled milk-glass lamps burning whale-oil or lard-oil, were stood inside large glass hurricane shades to protect the flame from drafts. Camphene, a new burning fluid compounded of turpentine and alcohol, made a dazzling flame but was dangerously explosive.

The Complete Cookery

Cookstoves were edging into the kitchen. The common sort was an iron top and front installed in the fireplace, the smoke going up the chimney. Another type was a round-bodied coal burner looking like a drum set up on three legs, which had a rotary top worked by a crank so that any pot or kettle could be pulled around handy to the stir spoon. Many people, however, preferred the hearth cookery they were accustomed to. Even the new cookbook, *The Complete Cookery*, ignored the stove, and gave recipes suited to the great brick oven, to the pot swinging on its crane, to the gridiron set above the embers.

The housewife was urged to be up at crack of day so that her bread sponge might not sour with long standing and so that time might be allowed for the two kneadings, two risings, and the full hour in the brick oven that insured fine-grained tender loaves. Good soup demanded a daylight start too. "Hang the soup pot over the fire at six in the morning if you dine at two o'clock."

Directions for making gelatin began, "Boil calves' feet in water." Turn a few pages and read the first steps to a cup of hot chocolate: "Roast the cocoa beans in a frying pan, clear them of husks, pound them in an iron mortar. Flavor with cinnamon and sugar."

Bread and cake recipes mostly called for "emptins" or home-made yeast to raise the dough. But a teaspoonful of pearl ash, obtained from wetting and refining wood ashes, and dissolved in a little vinegar, was best to raise a thin batter cake.

To freeze ice cream: "Pack down the tin container of cream in a tub of ice and salt for 1 hour; open up and beat with a paddle for 20 minutes; freeze for another hour; open up for another beating; let stand in ice for another 2 hours."

The Great Pain Reliever

Cookbooks usually contained a few pages of "Diet for the Sick." Often there was a section of simple household remedies: "Give a teaspoonful of turpentine and twenty drops of pep-permint for the colic . . . Roast an onion and bind it warm upon the ear to stop the ear-ache."

The doctor's standard treatments were a mustard plaster at the nape of the neck for a headache, daily doses of quinine for the ague shakes, and a bleeding for practically everything else. In a bloodletting the important thing was not the quantity of blood drawn, but the effect on the patient. The bleeding must continue till the patient fainted from loss of blood.

Vaccination as a preventive for smallpox was coming more and more into use. A scab plucked from the arm of a vacci-nated person was handily carried in the doctor's coat pocket. With the same knife that he had used to cut his plug of chew-ing tobacco, the doctor would pare off a bit of the scab, make a slight incision in the arm of the next patient, and insert the paring. The knife and the scab were thrust back into the pocket—with never a worry about bacteria.

No one was doing any worrying about bacteria. The mumps, measles, chicken pox, and scarletina were ills that everyone had to suffer, so it was thought best to get done with them early.

Mothers were advised to send their little ones to kiss a sick playmate and contract the contagion.

Epidemics of yellow fever now and again broke out in the port cities. Typhus fever and malaria took their toll of human life. But these paled into nothingness before the horror plague of 1832. In that year the Asiatic cholera reached America, spread with fearful swiftness. City after city awakened to the dread morning cry, "Bring out your dead." Within their houses people shuddered at the ghastly rattle of the death carts on the cobblestones. No one knew how to cure, or even check the disease. Some doctors gave doses of carbonate of soda every hour, others prescribed gum camphor, laudanum, and red pepper. All watched helplessly while their patients passed from violent purging and vomiting spells to cramps, intense thirst, heat within, cold sweats without, then the languor of exhaustion and death. A survivor recorded in his journal:

Multitudes that began the day in good health were corpses before sunset. Persons were found dead all along the street. Business ceased. Every dray, cart and carriage was employed in the transportation of corpses. There was no time for mourning; the living scarce had strength to bury their dead.

For days the plague raged, then was terminated as swiftly as it had begun. But not before it had numbered its victims by the thousands.

Out of a medical students' prank—the sniffing of ether fumes to send them off on wild jags of laughing and silly antics—was to grow the most momentous medical discovery of the century. The observation that no pain was suffered from bump or bruise during an ether jag led to the discovery of ether as the great pain reliever. In March, 1842, Dr. Crawford Long of Georgia administered ether to a patient and removed a small cystic tumor from the neck. No pain was felt, and no harm followed. In October, 1846, Dr. William Morton, a dentist, gave a successful public demonstration of ether anesthesia at the Massachusetts General Hospital.

Pain relief was proven. But it was far from being accepted. Because of ether's association with the ether jags, temperance societies denounced "etherization" as a form of intoxication. Tales were spread of the terrible aftereffects of ether. The doctors themselves were unhappily certain that sooner or later ether would kill a patient. So, for the time, the blessing of ether was denied. And men, strapped to a table for an operation, died in agony because the knife slipped in the midst of their uncontrollable struggles.

The First Coeds

New ideas about schools, schoolhouses, and schoolbooks were causing quite a stir. The title of Schoolmaster, one who masters or rules, must give way to Schoolteacher, one who teaches or explains. The noisy "blab method" of studying lessons in a loud whisper must cease. Schoolhouses must be made comfortable. Delightful new books must lead, not force, the young scholar into the pathway of knowledge.

One-room district schools were furnished with a wall blackboard on which to demonstrate arithmetic problems. Town schools hastened to replace the old backless benches with factory-made desk benches consisting of a cast-iron frame with folding seat, a back to lean against, and a shelf on which to rest books and papers.

From the nation's printing presses poured a flood of textbooks that were bright with pictures and lively with jingles. A merry *Musical Alphabet* started toddlers to singing:

> A is for Apple, Archer and Arrow,
> B is for Bull, a Bear and a Barrow,
> C for a Cat, and D for a Dish,
> E for an Egg, and F for a Fish.

Peter Parley's Geography (1829) opened with a verse:

> The world is round and like a ball
> Seems swinging in the air,
> A sky extends around it all,
> And stars are shining there.

Colburn's Arithmetic (1821) suggested using beans and nuts instead of abstract figures to teach small children addition and subtraction. Its insistence on oral class work with numbers marked the end of the old-fashioned "cyphering-book." The first of *McGuffey's Eclectic Readers* appeared in 1836, and five others followed within a decade. Offering a treasure of proverbs, dialogues, poems, and little tales stressing politeness, honesty, truth-telling and temperance, these entertained as well as instructed. Through the "Fable of the Tortoise" young readers were taught the value of patient persistence:

> "Plain, plodding people, we often shall find,
> Will leave hasty, confident people behind."

"Perfect ladies" were still being turned out by the fancy-work-for-females type of boarding schools. But farsighted educators were urging that girls be taught to use their minds instead of merely using their hands. Oberlin College in newly-settled Ohio went a bold step farther and gave America her first coeds. In 1837 four young women, having passed through the preparatory department, entered the college in company with thirty young men—all of them soberly intent on reading the Scriptures in the Greek and Hebrew originals.

Elsewhere college remained the exclusive property of young men. The college year ran from the first Monday in October to the third Monday in July, with three recitations a day, and Saturday a half-holiday. Each student furnished his room with a table, chair, bed, and bed-linen, and supplied his share of "firewood and candles". For board at two dollars a week all the students ate together at commons, and all complained bit-

terly of "tough boiled beef, watery coffee and worse cider."
In pleasant weather students might entertain themselves with
"jumping, wrestling and throwing quoits," but there was no
program of athletic exercises. Pent-up energy exploded in such
pranks as rolling logs downstairs in the night, and in "smoking
segars" on the sly. In an effort to discourage the fashion for
dueling, students were forbidden to carry "dirks, sword-canes
or other deadly weapons." Twice a week the library room
was opened and students were called by classes to borrow
books.

The Gift Book

> "Go! lovely volume, grace our Beauty's bowers,
> Improve her heart, amuse her listless hours."

Fashion approved the gift book as a New Year's, Christmas,
or anniversary offering from a gentleman to his ladylove.
Small volumes, handsomely bound in crimson or mauve mo-
rocco embossed in gold, were titled *The Album, The Souvenir, Friendship's Wreath*. Their pages were "enriched by
delicate sentiments in prose and poetry."

More to the masculine taste were tall tales and humorous
character sketches. Men in frock coats and plaid pants split
their sides laughing over *Major Jones's Courtship*, or *The
Biglow Papers*.

Newspaper readers gobbled up a mixture of national affairs,
political satire in dialect, temperance reports, and news of
wars, murders, and foreign visitors. Reports on the Mexican
War required two weeks by horseback courier to reach
eastern cities. Only a few years later, in columns headed "By
Magnetic Telegraph," newspapers were dishing out the news
with lightning-speed service.

Magazine readers found relaxation or information in such

dissimilar periodicals as: *Godey's Lady's Book, The Saturday Evening Post, The Dial, The Southern Quarterly Review, The North American Review, Peterson's Magazine,* and *Graham's Magazine.* Certain magazines specialized in political controversy, extracts from travelers' journals and reports on scientific experiments; others offered an "elegant variety" of hand-tinted fashion plates, songs with music, romantic tales and poems. Every week *The Youth's Companion* brought "stories and sermons, verses and conundrums."

Booksellers stocked everything from the *Edinburgh Encyclopediae* to story books for children. A low table displayed stacks of small, flat books titled in gilt, *Lucy and Rollo, The Clergyman's Orphan.* With only a glance at these prim stories of angelic babes who died young, of naughty lads who lived to sink, unwept, into drunkards' graves, youthful purchasers pounced upon the exciting adventures of the *Swiss Family Robinson.*

Grown-ups lingered over the display on the poetry table—Mr. Poe's *Raven,* Mr. Longfellow's *Evangeline,* Mr. Whittier's *Voices of Freedom.* They dipped into Mr. Cooper's novels of American characters in American settings—*The Pioneers, The Last of the Mohicans, The Pathfinder.* Meeting the demand for other yarns based upon America's past were *The Yemassee* by Mr. Simms, and *Horse Shoe Robinson* by Mr. Kennedy. For more solid information about their country they went to Miss Willard's or Mr. Bancroft's *History of the United States.*

The Riddle Flower and the Naughty Polka

A book that gave much pleasure was *The American Girl's Book,* published in 1831. From first page to last this chunky little volume was filled with games, puzzles, riddles, and other delightful amusements. Clever girls especially enjoyed preparing a bouquet of riddle flowers according to the book's directions: "Cut petals from pretty colored paper, pen a riddle on the top-side, the answer on the bottom-side, shape into a flower, and fasten to a wire stem. Such a bouquet makes a handsome ornament to the parlor table, and the riddles, if well chosen, are most entertaining to visitors." A riddle quite suited to lace-curtained parlors was: "When is a bonnet not a bonnet? (Answer: When it becomes a lady.)" Pioneers pushing the frontiers westward made up their own riddles as they rested around the camp fire: "How many cow-tails would it take to reach from Maine to the Mississippi? (Answer: One, if it was long enough.)"

For years American boys had been batting balls and racing around fields in games of Rounders and Baseball. Now some fresh twists were given to Baseball. The playing field was marked off in a diamond shape with four flat stones for bases, a round bat took the place of the flat paddle, and the number of players was limited to nine on each side. Instead of the old ruling that the first side to get one hundred runs was the winner, the game was set at nine innings.

New lively dances, the mazurka, galopade, polka, were sweeping the country—and raising a storm. Mamma fell into a faint and papa bellowed in his beard when daughter did the polka.

> Slide—glide—the Left Foot so,
>> Bound on the point of the Right Foot's toe;
> Now the Left in a heel-to-floor click,
>> Back with the Right in a good high kick.

Never did a dance leave such a trail of delight or fury as did the gay "heel, toe, and away we go" of the polka. Sweeping across Europe and on to America, it kicked up a row wherever it went. Its hop-skip certainly made the petticoats swing and show the ankles, but its rhythm was irresistible. It gave its name to the polka jacket and to polka dots adorning silks and ribbons. Quadrille and waltz, reels and rounds were all but overshadowed by the naughty polka.

Banjo Opera

A theatrical entertainment that drew the crowds was the blackface minstrel show, or banjo opera, as some called it. Burnt-cork-complexioned white actors furnished a merry evening of jokes, dialect songs, banjo picking, and buck dancing. The troupe lined up for a "walk around" song, "Step along Miss Lucy, step along Miss Lucy Long"; then a lively "wheel-about and turn-about" to the tune of "Jump, Jim Crow". Finally, to bang of tambourines and plunk-a-plunk of banjos, the soloist led off and everybody knocked down on the refrain:

> "Hey, git along, git along Josey,
> Hey, git along, Jim along Joe."

The catchy minstrel tunes, along with "gems from the composers," hymns, and ballads, were played and sung in the home. The great golden harp was falling into disfavor before the improved grand pianoforte which extended the five-octave keyboard both upward and downward. Two styles were equally popular, the heavy-legged square piano and the tall piano that stood flat against the wall like a bookcase. Seated on a revolving piano chair, with candles glowing on a stand, the pianist could choose the stirring "Washington March", the romantic "Meet Me By Moonlight", "The Yellow Rose of Texas", "Home, Sweet Home", or "Hark, Hark the Soft Bugle" with its charming bugle and echo effects.

This was a tuneful time. Even the temperance societies were taking a try at whipping Old Demon Rum with music. Wearers of "the white ribbon" gathered in front of saloons to sing:

"Our youthful hearts with Temp'rance burn,
From dram-shops we your steps would turn.
Away, away the bowl."

The canal boatman sang:

"I got a mule, her name is Sal.
Fifteen miles on the Erie Canal."

The wagoners, whom the iron horses were cutting out of their jobs, had a song too, a doleful song:

"Oh, once I made money by driving my team,
But the goods are now hauled on the railroad by steam."

Folks pushing westward across the plains to California gold fields sang when they had the breath to spare. A favorite on the covered wagon trail was "Oh, Susanna". More true, alas, was "On the Banks of the Sacramento":

"There's plenty of gold, so I've been told,
On the banks of the Sacramento.

"There's plenty of bones amid the stones,
On the banks of the Sacramento."

Chapter 8

FAMILY QUARREL (1850-74)

"Then let our Southern States separate and depart in peace."
—John C. Calhoun

"Physically speaking, we cannot separate."
—Abraham Lincoln

HOT WORDS flew like brickbats. "Slave drivers! Owners of human flesh." "Hypocrites! See that your own hands are clean!" Men rushed about making speeches; women in hoop skirts and men in top hats listened to the speeches; newspapers printed them. Harriet Beecher Stowe published a book titled *Uncle Tom's Cabin, or, Life Among the Lowly.* People shed tears when they read it.

Undoubtedly there were certain ills of humanity that needed righting. In the industrial districts of the nation millions of poor whites—men, women, and thin-faced children—were practically slaves to their factory jobs. They did dawn-to-dark drudgery at the machines, received a pittance of pay, lived under squalid conditions. Theirs, however, was less obvious slavery that must wait three-quarters of a century before it was to end. On the wide-spreading plantations to the southward were millions of black folk who were actually slaves. They tilled the soil for their white masters. They belonged to their masters as if they were cattle to be worked or sold off at their owner's will. This was a terrible wrong, and it needed changing. But the South wasn't ready to change, for it needed the slaves to chop and pick cotton.

"The Negro slaves must be free," cried the North.

"The slaves are our property," retorted the South.

While tempers flared north and south, the West was rising on a golden tide. California was made a state in 1850, Minnesota followed in 1858 and Oregon in 1859. This was the year the first oil well was dug in Pennsylvania. This was also the year of John Brown's raid into Virginia to stir up the slaves into rebellion against their masters. John Brown was hanged, but he'd emphasized the cry, "The slaves must be free."

This cry against slavery was a battle brand to fire men's passions. But deep underneath smoldered the jealous rivalry between two modes of life, between the slow-moving plantation South and the hustling-bustling North. Little by little, through the years, the country had been separating into a southern half and a northern half, into an agricultural section and an industrial section. Now came an open break. The eleven Southern states, from Virginia to Texas, seceded from the Union and formed the Confederate States of America, with Jefferson Davis as their president. Abraham Lincoln, who had been inaugurated President of the United States, declared that no state could lawfully leave the Union, that he would enforce the laws of the Union in the seceding states, and hold the forts within them.

War was at hand!

The clash came April 12, 1861, with the firing upon Fort Sumter. Then the Battle of Bull Run—and on into four years of horror. Families were divided—brother fought against brother. Armies stormed back and forth across the land. Food crops were destroyed; homes, barns, iron foundries, railroads, and bridges were burned or blown up. Men in Union blue or Confederate gray marched, fought, died. Anxious-faced women, wherever they were, rolled bandages, nursed the wounded, tried to forget heartache in work.

A population of twenty-two million in the North stood against a mere nine million people in the South. More battles followed: more guns, more men in blue rushed against the thin gray line of the desperate Confederacy. A bold blue line pressed in on Vicksburg on the Mississippi. A blue line pushed forward in Virginia. Surrender came, at Appomattox; the war was over: the North had won.

Reconstruction began its agony. The South was a conquered land under a military government. In many places cattle and hogs had been killed or carried off, homes and farm buildings burned, cotton gins and grist mills destroyed. The old magnificence of the plantations was gone. Weary soldiers in ragged gray uniforms returned home to start farming on a small scale.

For the Negro freedmen, life was still not easy. Now they must provide their own food, clothing, shelter; must earn a place for themselves in this land of America.

The Union added four new states: Kansas in 1861; West Virginia, 1863; Nevada, 1864; and Nebraska, 1867. In this same year, 1867, the government in Washington bought the far northern territory of Alaska from Russia for the sum of seven million dollars in gold.

All over the country men were throwing themselves into work, intent on making up for the lost war years, intent on making themselves rich as fast as possible. They were hurrying, wasting resources, grabbing while the grabbing was good. Iron, lead, tin, gold, and silver were feverishly dug from the earth. Forests were cut into timber, hills burned into brick, mountains quarried for stone. Factory workers were driven harder than ever to fill carload orders for cheap furniture, china dishes, tinware, cookstoves, sewing machines.

On the plains the Indian and the buffalo were making their last stand against swarming settlers, guns, wagon trains, and bellowing herds of domestic cattle. Here was the Wild West where cowboys in shaggy chaps, with lariats coiled around saddle horns, rode bucking broncos; where two-gun sheriffs shot down bullying bad men.

The first oil well had been dug in 1859. "Oil! Oil!" sounded the exultant shout as the thick yellowish-green foam gushed up in hundreds of other drill pipes. Men poured into the Pennsylvania oil region. Derricks of heavy timber straddled the countryside. Shanties popped up, saloons and dance halls followed; then stores, banks, shops. In a few months a village would be oil-boomed into a city. The oil was put to many uses—medicine, lamp oil, lubricant for rolling wheels.

Now the whistle of the steam locomotive was heard in every section of the nation. Irish laborers, along with the Swedes, Germans, Italians, and every other strong-armed immigrant who could swing a pick, were working on the railroad. In two and a half years they built over twenty thousand miles of railway in the United States.

New cities sprouted and grew. Old cities erected impressive brownstone and marble public buildings. Conveniences were multiplying. Gas was common for illuminating purposes, and coal for fuel. In a few cities, waterworks were beginning to supplant the pump and well.

There were no gas lights or running water in the crowded, dingy quarters of the city's laboring classes. Farm and village

1. Titusville oil well. 2. The death of Lincoln. 3. Building the Capitol. 4. Wagon train west!

families continued to draw water at the well and lug it in by the bucketful. Lighting came from tallow candles or oil lamps. At the village store the male population relaxed over a game of checkers, argued politics, reached into the cracker barrel for a free lunch, and developed the peculiarly American "cracker barrel wit" of the tall tale:

"Shucks, that ain't nothing. Our mosquitoes grow big as jaybirds. To git away from 'em, Paw crawled under Maw's new wash pot. But them danged pests poked their bills right through the iron and flew off with the pot."

Horses and mules pulled the farmers' plows and wagons; pulled the streetcars on tracks down city streets. Only well-to-do families kept horses and a carriage and had a stable and carriage house at the rear of their lot. These same well-to-do families furnished their big two-story, mansard-roofed, Gothic-towered homes with elaborately machine-carved black walnut parlor suites. There were dining room suites, and bedroom suites with marble tops on bureaus and washstands. The servant problem was not very pressing, not with so many Irish and German girls arriving by every ship. Mamma wore a chignon and a bustle, and was enormously proud of her sewing machine that could run up a seam in a flash. She superintended the cleaning, helped make desserts, did most of the marketing and a great deal of planning to get the girls married off. Papa wore mutton-chop whiskers, a black Prince Albert coat, and exercised his authority as head of the house. He didn't hesitate, either, to march an ornery boy off to the woodshed for a session with the strap, despite reproachful looks from mamma and loud yells from the boy.

Daily and weekly newspapers kept folks up to date on national and world happenings. They read of the laying of the Atlantic cable; of the horrors of the Chicago fire that burned for three days and sent 300,000 people fleeing for their lives. Masculine readers thought it mighty fine for Miss Clara Barton to found the American Red Cross, but they shook their heads over the determination women were showing in their women's rights movement, and in the Women's Christian Temperance Union. Strong-minded females were not only singing hymns outside barrooms and swinging hatchets at whisky barrels, but were demanding the right to vote just as if they were the equals of men.

Seven years after the end of the war that had almost split the country into two separate nations, a Peace Jubilee was musically celebrated in Boston. Opera singers and orchestras were brought from abroad. America assembled twenty-nine crack brass bands, a grand chorus of seventeen thousand voices, an orchestra of five hundred violins, with other instruments in proportion. There was a mammoth drum that measured thirty-six feet across and a cannon to produce stunning effects during the singing of the battle hymns. But the Peace Jubilee opened upon a note of magnificent solemnity. Twenty thousand people stood together and lifted voices in "Old Hundred":

> "From all that dwell below the skies,
>   Let the Creator's praise arise."

Secession Pudding versus Union Pie

Americans liked things big. Especially they liked fine big dinners served in numerous courses. The decade before the Civil War was a period of glorified cookery. At a public dinner to honor some important person or event, guests sat down to a feast that began with soup, two kinds of fish, five meat fancies, seventeen entrees; then worked on through roast goose, roast duck, roast turkey, twenty vegetables, twelve desserts, and ended on wine, cigars, speeches, and toothpicks.

Private entertaining was almost as elaborate. Fashionable

urs for eating were two o'clock dinner, five o'clock social tea, eleven o'clock supper. To improve its flavor a ham might be soaked in cider for three weeks, stuffed with sweet potatoes, baked in maple syrup. Cake recipes began, "Take twenty eggs . . ."

The Civil War put an end to all this. Food prices soared. In the blockaded South flour cost $250 per barrel in Confederate money, tea $35 the pound. Housewives brewed okra-seed coffee and corn-fodder tea. Sugar became so scarce that some children reached the age of four or five years without ever tasting it. Recipes were developed to use what materials came to hand. The Southerner's "Secession Pudding" and "Jeff Davis Cake" were balanced by "Union Pie" and "Yankee Cake".

In the armies of both North and South there was suffering from scurvy because of lack of fresh vegetables. "Send us onions," the soldiers begged in their letters home. Army fare was salt beef, hardtack, and black coffee.

The return to peace set housewives to restocking their pantry shelves. Meats were smoked, salted, and potted—that is, cooked till tender, pounded to a paste, and stored in stone crocks or pots. Eggs were soaked in lime water, packed away in sawdust. Commercial packers were putting up food in tin cans, but housewives preferred glass jars and the time-proven "pound of sugar to pound of fruit" method. From May to November kitchens wafted their spicy tang of boiling juices, as berries, peaches, plums, were made into jellies and jams.

Manufacturers were advertising a "patent freezer turned by a crank" to speed up ice-cream making. Another handy item was a "zinc lined ice chest." Housewives were quite willing to go kitchen-adventuring with the cookstove. The newest cookbooks published recipes for quick hot breads to be baked in the oven of an iron stove. Instead of such out-of-date leavening as pearl ash, the cookbooks recommended the new portable yeast, a blend of soda and cream of tartar, "with which bread is easily made, requires little labor, no kneading or waiting for dough to rise."

The Wounded Are Coming

Doctors warned that too many big dinners with too much wine and too many rich pastries would bring on the gout— which was a very painful ailment marked by "headache, nausea, numbness in the limbs and a burning pain in the great toe." There wasn't much to do about the gout except to recommend that the patient eat less and exercise more. Sufferers from the gout, however, and from other afflictions, were enthusiastically dosing themselves on the new "patent medicines". Advertisements in almanacs, and posters pasted on barn doors, urged the public to buy health by the bottle and pillbox.

Even before the war, intubation or insertion of a silver tube into the throat to save a diphtheria patient from choking to death proved successful. The clinical thermometer, and the newly invented hypodermic syringe, clumsy but effective, began to be put to widespread use. And at last ether, as the great anesthetic, won acceptance. Now that a patient could be put into a deep sleep by a whiff of ether, the era of real surgery dawned. Then war struck, and it seemed as if relief of pain had been perfected at the moment the nation needed it most. But, alas, little ether was to be had.

Behind the battle lines sounded the cry, "The wounded are coming!" Wagons creaked to the rear, jolting their gruesome loads. In makeshift hospitals, men who had been fighting for days in rain and mud were bedded down, row upon row, on the floor. Surgeons, orderlies, and a few women nurses did what they could. All medical supplies were scarce: no antiseptic to stem the horror tide of gangrene, seldom any chloroform or ether to dull the agony of an amputation, no quinine.

For camp diarrhea, measles, typhoid, malaria, the fevers were just dosed with brew of willow bark.

Mothers put their faith in a bit of vile-smelling asafetida tied in a bag about the neck to ward off colds and coughs. The doctor was called in to set broken bones, to vaccinate in the event of a smallpox scare, to burn out a mad-dog bite with a hot iron or lunar caustic. He held to the theory that pus in a wound was "natural," and certainly was not connected with the fact that he performed operations in his frock coat, with his silk-threaded needles stuck handily into the lapel. The English surgeon, Lister, was of a different opinion. Convinced that pus in a wound was due "not to the infected air, but to bacteria passed from the unclean hands of surgeon and wound-dresser," Lister, in 1867, announced his principle of antisepsis:

The material which I have employed is Carbolic Acid, the most powerful antiseptic with which we are at present acquainted. I am prepared to go so far as to say that a solution of Carbolic Acid in twenty parts of water, while a mild and cleanly application, may be relied on to destroy any septic germs that may fall upon the wound during an operation.

From Crinolines to Bustles

While doctors denounced tight lacing as injurious to female health, a ladies' magazine edited by a Mrs. Amelia Bloomer came out in favor of a "sensible" costume that consisted of an uncorseted bodice over ankle-length "bloomers" and knee-length skirt. A few daring "bloomer girls" appeared in public in the new costume but they speedily weakened under the jibes men cast at them and returned to sweeping skirts and hour-glass waists.

But corset strings continued to be pulled tight to help ladies achieve the fashionably small waist. Sleeve puffs vanished before the new admiration for sloping shoulders. Enormously wide skirts were held out by wire hoops or by a crinoline petticoat of stiffened haircloth. Stylish wraps were the bell-sleeved sacque and the cape-sleeved dolman. Flat hats vied for favor with bonnets. Hair was parted in the middle and brushed smoothly over the ears, or dressed in a "waterfall" and confined in a chenille net at the back of the head.

Pioneer wives were as tight-bodiced and full-skirted as their stay-at-home sisters, but materials were chosen for durability, and a cotton sunbonnet shielded the head. Pioneer husbands were sensibly garbed in warm jacket, checked cotton shirt, woolen trousers tucked into high boots.

The war, of course, put American men into uniform, either Union blue or Confederate gray. Clothing was plentiful in the North where textile mills were booming and ports were open to trade, but the South, with its ports blockaded by Yankee gunboats, felt the pinch of war. Women organized "needle battalions" to sew uniforms, girls were set to knitting socks. Discarded spinning wheels and hand looms were brought down from attics, homegrown cotton was woven into cloth, dyes were concocted from roots and berries. If a blockade runner managed to slip his craft past enemy lines there seemed no limit to the prices he demanded in Confederate paper money: "Calico $10 a yard; a French merino or mohair dress $800; Cloak of fine cloth $1,000; Balmoral boots $250; French gloves $125 the pair."

At the end of the war men got back into black broadcloth, into brown and drab worsteds. Less impressive than the snug-waisted, full-skirted frock coat and top hat outfit was the short sack coat rounded at bottom, buttoned high, and worn with a soft felt hat or a bowl-shaped derby. Trousers were wide and baggy. Stylish gentlemen emphasized such elegancies as a stiff linen collar and carelessly knotted silk tie, a gold watch chain draped across the midriff, and fine-flowing whiskers variously known as sideburns, side bats and mutton chops.

Small boys sported velvet sacques and wide trousers to below the knee. Small girls wore hoop skirts. To protect baby's long petticoats, mamma could now buy rubberized "water-proof diapers" to button over the frequently inadequate cotton variety.

After centuries of laborious hand sewing, relief came at last to needle-pricked home seamstresses. From stitching canvas for sailing ships the sewing machine had passed to stitching men's suits in tailor shops. Now women were permitted the benefit of its flying needle. Another fine new thing was the ready-cut paper pattern.

A few years after the end of the war, the fashion for bell-shaped crinoline skirts fell before the popularity of the bustle. Advertised as "the elegant skirt-improver", this bustle was a cage-like affair of whalebone or wire applied to the rear of the feminine form. It was guaranteed to "support twenty yards of drapery."

The Black Walnut Parlor Suite

The descendants of families that had settled down to housekeeping in a white-columned Greek temple were now happily settling down to housekeeping in mansions modeled after some peak-roofed Gothic cathedral. The dignity of tall white columns was discarded for the romantic charm of towers, turrets, ornamental chimney pots, and piazzas balustraded in factory-made cast-iron curlicues.

Interior arrangements provided romantic nooks and odd-shaped rooms. Nobody gave a thought to wasted space. Popular taste approved lavish adornment—tall mirrors in gilt frames, window curtains fringed and draped, scroll trim on tall dark furniture, and cold marble tops on tables and bureaus. A high-backed cast-iron chair was an appropriate item for the reception hall. Fine city homes were lighted by flaming gas jets in bronze-and-crystal chandeliers suspended from plaster ceiling rosettes. Ignorant servants, however, had to be warned to "turn off the gas. Don't blow it out."

Now that factories were turning out all sorts of machine-made goods at prices people could afford to pay, more families were fixing up their homes with the soft carpets and shiny furniture that only rich people had been able to buy when everything had to be made by hand. Often the factory-made articles were not as smoothly finished or as artistically designed as the old-time handcraft articles, but even so they were a forward step toward comforts and conveniences for everybody instead of for the few. For the price of a single hand-made chair a housewife could now fill a room with furniture, so suites or matched sets became the fashion. For parlor, dining room, or bedroom nothing was deemed so handsome as a black walnut suite in pointed-Gothic style. Included, of course, was a lady chair, armless, and suitably shaped to accommodate hoop skirts.

In the big cities where public waterworks were piping water right into one's house, the finest new houses had bathrooms.

Washstands were fitted with elegant marble tops having fixed basins sunk in them. Water closets were designed with square boxseats of panelled and varnished wood. Oblong tin or zinc tubs were similarly enclosed in panelling. Hot water was piped from a waterback attached to the kitchen stove, which was a most comfortable provision in winter weather.

High School

The big new high school had pointed-Gothic windows, a Gothic tower—and it was built at the taxpayer's expense. A

purely American product, the high school was an expansion
upward of the district school idea of free education for all,
girls as well as boys being admitted. A classical course, em-
phasizing Latin and Greek, was college preparatory. An English course included "composition and rhetoric, history, alge-
bra, bookkeeping, and the sciences." Like the college, the
four-year course was divided into freshman, sophomore,
junior, and senior years. Unlike the academy, there were no
elementary classes.

Lower schools divided sharply into city and country
schools. The city favored huge buildings, a staff of teachers,
many of them women, and rows of varnished desk seats in
high-ceilinged classrooms. Country schools ranged from neat,
red-painted frame buildings to crude log-cabin affairs limited
to one short term and the Three R's. In the better schools a
graded system was being tried out—eight grades below high
school. School opened with a reading from the Bible; the
spelling class stood to recite; the arithmetic class went to the
blackboard; the reading class opened their *McGuffey's Eclectic Readers*. Store-bought copybooks and steel pens were used
for the writing lesson.

Jolly new textbooks had a song for every subject. The
grammar song gave a verse about each of the nine parts of
speech, as:

> "Verbs tell of something to be done,
>   To read, write, count, sing, jump, run."

The geography song not only rhymed islands, mountains,
rivers, and states, but named the state capitals as well:

> "In Alabama see a new and cotton-growing state,
>   And at Montgomery, we find, its law-makers debate."

War struck hard at the country's colleges. In the South
college buildings were burned, libraries scattered. In both

North and South students rushed from the campus to the army camp. With the return to peace, higher education began again its slow forward march. The peak of the public school system was the state university, largely supported by land grants, and, in the West, open to both young men and young women, though the women were few. An act of Congress also provided land grants for an agricultural and mechanical college in each state. Now the idea of courses adapted to the student's needs, rather than one traditional classical course required of all, began to gain favor. The need of physical exercise was finally acknowledged by school authorities. Ladders, bars, and wooden horses were set up in gymnasiums. An intercollegiate boat race in 1852 and a baseball match in 1858 were the beginnings of college athletics. Literary societies, debating societies, and Greek letter fraternities cultivated college spirit.

Vassar, founded in 1865, was a college for women, "with women professors." The curriculum included Greek, Latin, moral philosophy, and "calisthenics practiced in a Calisthenium." But no needlework.

Dime Novels

One could draw the curtains, light the lamp, pull a chair to the fire, and settle down to a quiet evening at home with a volume of solid worth. There was Motley's *Rise of the Dutch Republic*, Holmes's *Autocrat of the Breakfast Table*, Emerson's *Essays*, Thoreau's *Walden*, Whitman's *Leaves of Grass*, or *Hiawatha*, Mr. Longfellow's poem based on Indian myths. If one wanted a novel, there was Mr. Melville's *Moby Dick*, or Mr. Hawthorne's *The Scarlet Letter*.

Hoop-skirted females wept their way through *The Wide Wide World* by Miss Warner, *The Lamplighter* by Miss Cummins, *Beulah* and *Inez* by Mrs. Wilson, and other novels about friendless orphans, lost lovers, and gentle heroines too good for this earth.

Malaeska: The Indian Wife of the White Hunter was published in 1860, and was advertised as "A Dollar Book for a Dime." This was the first dime novel, and it was from the "accomplished pen of the celebrated Mrs. Ann Stephens." The dime novels arrived just in time to furnish reading matter to Civil War soldiers. By the wagonload the little books were sent to the front, and often enough white flags of truce were raised while messengers crossed enemy lines to swap *The Raftsman's Daughter* for *The Privateers' Cruise*, or *The Captives of the Frontier* for *Oonomoo the Huron*. The horrors of war were forgotten while "brave wilderness scouts crept through the underbrush, blood-curdling shrieks rent the air and treacherous redskins bit the dust."

Every section of the country was represented in books. *Surry of Eagle's Nest* was a story of the recent war from the Southern point of view. *The Hoosier Schoolmaster* told of "lickin' and larnin' " in the Indiana backwoods. *Luck of Roaring Camp* had a far Western mining camp for its setting.

Young readers found delight in the magic make-believe of *Alice in Wonderland*. They raced for the silver skates with *Hans Brinker*. And four daughters in any family had frequent spells of trying to lead lives like Meg, Jo, Beth, and Amy of Miss Alcott's beloved *Little Women*.

Clipper Round the Horn

Books, journals, and letters to newspapers recorded the Forty-Niners' mad rush to the California gold fields. This rush to the West continued. A high-masted clipper ship doing the sixteen thousand miles around Cape Horn was still the fastest way to get there. In very truth the chanteyman sang:

"A yankee ship coming down the river,
Her sails of silk, her masts of silver."

The American clipper was the sailing ship brought to perfection—the hull sharpened and raking boldly forward, the towering masts strung with ten thousand yards of canvas. *Lightning, Challenge, Comet*—their very names spelled speed. The times demanded speed. Tea clippers raced from China with cargoes of tea, spices, and silks. Gold clippers whisked gold-bedazzled men around the tip of South America and up to California. A little paddle-wheel steamer made the run around the Horn in three hundred days. The *Flying Cloud* clipped the time to 89 days and 21 hours. Another clipper sped from Boston to Liverpool in 12 days and 6 hours, the fastest transatlantic crossing ever made by sailing ship.

Less picturesque than the gallant clippers, steamships were more dependable regarding departure and arrival. Steamers were shuttling the Atlantic in a 12- to 14-day schedule. Sailing packets divided passengers into "cabin, second-cabin and steerage," the latter made up of poor people who brought their own food and were crowded together in the dark, airless hold. Steamships carried no "steerage", as every inch of hold was needed to stock coal to fuel the engines. Passengers complained of the distressing odors of engine grease mingled with the side-to-side rocking motion of the paddle wheels. Ladies were often prostrated the entire voyage. But improvements were on the way. The paddle-wheeler lost out to the swifter screw-propelled liner; wooden hulls gave place to stronger and larger hulls of iron. The steamship, however, still looked like a sailing ship. Sails were raised fore and aft of the smokestack as master mariners clung to the thrifty policy of assisting the engines when a proper wind was to be had. Below deck was the grand saloon, with satin-upholstered sofas and oil lamps swinging in brass chandeliers. In each stateroom were two bunks, a washstand with tin basin and water jug, a wall mirror and candle lantern.

Despite storms and seasickness, an ocean voyage was less hazardous than a trip aboard a river steamer. The toll of river accidents was appalling. Half a hundred steamboats sunk on snags, exploded or burned in a single year. Hundreds of persons died—many of them sacrificed to high-pressure boilers and the irresistible challenge of a race. Passengers crowded to the rail to shout down a rival steamer. "Don't let it pass! Get up steam—set the fires to roaring! Throw on barrels of resin! Throw on slabs of fat meat!" Dangerous, yes. Still people swarmed aboard the steamboats to enjoy soft comforts and rich eating at low fares.

The overland rival to a clipper round the Horn was the covered wagon. In long caravans these lumbered westward. By ox-team from Missouri to California took half a year. In the wake of the wagons came the stage-coach. By 1857 the overland mail was operating between St. Louis and San Francisco, its coach relays covering the two thousand miles in less than thirty days. For a brief two years, 1860 and 1861, the Pony Express rushed the mail over this same distance in nine days.

City families who could not afford to keep a "carriage and pair" rode the horsecars on the street railway that ran right through the center of town. For a fare of twenty cents one sat on a plush seat (or a hard plank). When ready to alight, a sharp jerk on the strap, which ran through the car and was fastened around the driver's leg, gave the "stop" signal.

A journey behind a snorting steam locomotive was almost as dangerous as a trip on a river steamer. People exclaimed in horror over head-on collisions, cars derailed, bridges crashing down; then they bought more tickets and risked their necks

for the privilege of whizzing down an iron track at a speed
of thirty miles an hour.

On May 10, 1869, two powerful locomotives, one wheeling
westward on the Union Pacific, the other eastward on the
Central Pacific, met at Promontory Point, Utah. Tap-tap-tap:
DONE! over the telegraph wires the signal flashed to a waiting nation. The last spike, the golden spike from California,
had been driven into place. At last the vastness of America was
spanned by shining steel rails. By the end of the year passengers
were crossing the continent on railroad trains. There was some
waiting for connections and changing of cars, but a crossing
could be managed in six days.

Locomotives, whether coal-burners or wood-burners, had
evolved into iron monsters with cowcatcher, headlight, bell,
enclosed cab, and a wide-mouthed smokestack with a wire
screen across the top to hinder flying sparks. Now Mr. Pullman's new sleeping cars, hotel cars and dining cars—heated
by a hot air furnace under the floor and illuminated by pairs
of hanging oil lamps—created a new kind of luxury travel.

Waxworks and Wonders

There were so many sights to see that one needed ten pairs
of eyes. Mamma held small sister by the hand, and bade brother
keep close to them, as they pushed through the crowd that
had come to view the traveling museum's "great moral and
educational exhibitions." Here were true-to-life wax figures
of President Washington in cocked hat and knee breeches, of
Queen Victoria in crown and royal robes. Nearby were the
"new and colossal" panoramas, "The Burning of Moscow"
and "The Six Days of Creation", painted on five square miles
of canvas. Other attractions included "living skeletons, bearded
ladies, dancing dogs, petrified mermaids." But what everybody

wanted to see was the handsome and polite General Tom Thumb, billed as "the smallest man in the world."

Showboats plied the rivers and brought drama to far-off places. Red-wheeled circus vans transported "trapeze artists and fierce wild animals" over country roads. In New York City *The Black Crook*, a musical extravaganza with 150 high-kicking chorus girls, packed the theater every night.

A professional baseball club was organized. Football went intercollegiate. Roller skates were patented. Young ladies showed their steadiness of hand at Carpet Bowls, the china balls "rolling so prettily" across the carpeted parlor floor. But to swing the mallet in a game of croquet was a breath-taking performance for a girl with hand-span waist and skirts that swept the ground.

Dancing academies gave instruction in all the fashionable dances, "the new German cotillion, the lancers, the quadrille, waltz, polka, schottische." Dancing masters announced that they did not encourage the "hop and jump" style of schottische and polka, but the gay dancers jumped anyway, and the hoop skirts jumped with them.

Ballads: Tuneful and Tearful

Young people gathered around massive square pianos of rosewood or mahogany for evenings of social singing. Parlors resounded to the lilt of "De Camptown Races" and "Wait for the Wagon"; to the sweet melodies of "My Old Kentucky Home" and "Swanee River", to "Listen to the Mocking Bird", "My Darling Nelly Gray", and "Lilly Dale":

> Oh, Lilly, sweet Lilly, dear Lilly Dale,
> Now the wild rose blossoms
> O'er her little green grave,
> 'Neath the trees in the flow'ry vale.

During the Civil War, the roar of cannon, beat of drum, and thud of marching feet marked time to a swelling chorus. Men sang to keep their courage up. Those at home remembered them in song. In the North, voices lifted in the magnificent "Battle Hymn of the Republic". Lincoln's call for volunteers was answered with the ringing lines, "We Are Coming, Father Abraham, Three Hundred Thousand Strong", and "The Battle Cry of Freedom":

> "We'll rally round the flag, boys,
>   Rally once again,
>   Shouting the battle cry of freedom."

From the South sounded "The Cross of the South", "Melt the Bells", "Rebel, 'Tis a Holy Name", and the soul-stirring cry of "Dixie":

> "Southrons, hear your country call you!
> Up, lest worse than death befall you!
>   To arms! to arms! to arms! in Dixie!"

Finally, after four years of sorrow, Americans at last could sing, "The Cruel War Is Over", and "When Johnny Comes Marching Home Again". Singers turned gladly to the gentler airs of peace, to "Meet Me", "Josie, at the Gate", "In the Gloaming", and "Silver Threads among the Gold".

A brave little group of dark-skinned young singers, newly freed from slavery, were introducing their Negro spirituals to the white world. These were the Jubilee Singers from Fisk University, who sang their way through the North to raise money for their school. The songs themselves were prayers— "Go Down, Moses", "Roll, Jordan, Roll", and "I'll Hear the Trumpet Sound":

> You may bury me in the East,
> You may bury me in the West;

But I'll hear the trumpet sound
In that morning.
In that morning, my Lord,
How I long to go,
For to hear the trumpet sound
In that morning.

Chapter 9

HAPPY BIRTHDAY, U.S.A. (1875-99)

The Declaration of Independence—July 4, 1776
The Centennial Exposition—July 4, 1876

HAPPY BIRTHDAY to the one-hundred-year-old United States of America! Philadelphia, the city where the Liberty Bell had rung out its shout for freedom, gave a birthday party —a great centennial fair.

Everybody was invited to the party. The summer of the Centennial was a time of family groups coming from all over the country for a delightful get-together in Philadelphia. In six days and several changes of cars, the transcontinental railway brought people from San Francisco, from Boston by steamship, and others from Mississippi, part way by river steamer, part way by rail. From their farms twenty miles out of the city, families drove in their rockaways behind a pair of horses. Those in Philadelpia proper merely stepped aboard a horse-drawn street railway car and were out at the fair grounds in no time.

According to a booklet titled *Visitors' Guide*, there were "236 acres within the Main Exhibition enclosure." A complete narrow-gauge double-track steam railway system operated within the enclosure, and visitors were advised to take a seat in one of the cars for a quick first look at the whole show— cost, five cents. After that folks settled down to sight-seeing. Girls had fits over the "darling little Japanese house with grass mats to sit on"; boys had to be dragged past soda-water and popcorn stands. Women, very much dressed up in the newest-style bustle, glowed with pride over the women's pavilion, devoted entirely to exhibits of women's work. The men, mutton-chop whiskers bristling with determination, herded their families to the machinery hall to view the visible record of America's mechanical contributions to the world. People accustomed to the marvels of modern transportation had to smile as they gazed at the models of those first queer little steamboats, at the first railway cars shaped like stagecoaches. The crowd moved slowly past the Franklin stove and the lightning rod, past the nail machine, the cotton gin, the screw propeller. People looked their fill at reaper and harvester and magnetic telegraph, and exclaimed in awe to hear a distant voice come over Mr. Bell's telephone wire. Women waxed enthusiastic over the sewing machine, but ignored the type-writer, quite unaware of the effect it was to have on their lives. Men glanced at the rotary printing press, passed by a contraption called a motion picture machine, stared, entranced, at the Gatling gun and the Colt revolver.

The Centennial Exposition was a big success. Americans liked big things done in a big way. Proof of this was their thousand million dollars worth of railroads, and the newly completed Brooklyn Bridge. It cost fifteen million dollars to build, more than twice as much as was paid for the whole Territory of Alaska. Other evidence was the Statue of Liberty, a colossal bronze lady lifting her flaming torch three hundred feet into the sky as a beacon to the poor and oppressed of every land. America itself was big—a lusty giant of a nation that straddled a continent, one foot in the Atlantic, the other in the Pacific. The last census reported a population of over sixty million. A flood tide of immigration, of Poles, Germans, Italians, Scandinavians, was mixing people in the great melting pot that was America. Eight new states were in process of being added—Colorado in 1876; Washington, Montana, North Dakota, and South Dakota in 1889; Idaho and Wyoming in 1890; Utah in 1896—totaling forty-five states in all.

Oklahoma Territory, purchased from the Indians in 1889, was opened to white settlers in April of that year. Towns of tents and shanties sprang up in a day. The town of Guthrie, in four short months, achieved a population of eight thousand, with streetcars and electric lights.

America was using up its natural resources in a big way. Oil wells, mines, forests, and farm lands were ruthlessly stripped to make rich men richer. Industry was doing things in a ruthless way too. The village craftsman was fast disappearing. Factories made the shoes, the brooms, the wagon wheels that a few years back had been produced in local shops. Big oil companies were buying up lesser oil companies under threat of forcing them out of business. Steel and wheat, coal mining and meat packing, were developing into monopolies in the greedy hands of a few men who reaped fortunes from work of men and women laboring for low wages. Newly organized labor fought back with bloody strikes. Processions of strikers marched through city streets, demanded an eight-hour day, an increase in pay.

Mr. Edison put his electric light bulb on the market. The older generation backed off in horror from the queer little thing that looked like a red-hot hairpin stuck in a glass bottle. The idea of thinking it safe to run fire along one's ceilings inside of a wire was upsetting. Kerosene lamps were new-fangled enough.

But the world refused to stand still for the older generation. Next thing, telephones were being installed in private homes. Cities were busy stringing overhead wires; there was also a beginning of rural telephone lines. What a boon to lonely farm wives to be able to tinkle the phone bell, take down the receiver, and be in touch with another human voice. What a comfort to be able to call for help in case of sickness or fire.

People didn't take so enthusiastically to another mechanical marvel—a vehicle powered by a gasoline motor. Now and again the road was invaded by one of these "horseless car-riages" that emitted vile smells and noises as it whizzed along at nine miles per hour. The horse had long been king of the road, and the town livery stable touched family life in a variety of ways. Its rubber-tired traps were just right for taking your best girl riding. Its drays hauled the trunks of visiting kin to and from the railroad station. Its fringed-top surreys turned out for funerals and weddings.

Only one family in a hundred owned a horse and buggy, but plenty of married couples found $25 a week a very com-fortable income upon which to raise their children. Corn meal was priced at 20 cents a peck, bacon 9 cents a pound, ham 12½ cents, sugar 6½ cents. A dime would buy a dozen eggs or a pound of lard. Muslins and lawns cost 9 cents the yard, calico 5 cents. Neat black cotton stockings cost only 15 cents. For $12 one could purchase a sewing machine. As little as $27.50 would put an organ in the parlor, though it took all of $35 to

1. Brooklyn Bridge. 2. Queen Anne cottage. 3. Early automobile.
4. Remember the *Maine!*

acquire a really snappy model with carpeted pedals, carved lamp brackets, and a revolving stool. Men were on the job all day at the store, office, or on the farm; after supper they could relax on a velveteen-upholstered Morris chair to read the paper. Women enjoyed their display of souvenir coffee cups in the china cabinet, read an annual paper at the woman's club, and strove to rear their offspring properly.

Families were smaller than in colonial times, but the old adage about children being "seen and not heard" still held good. Strict parents forbade any playing of games on Sunday, but weekdays were lively with kite flying, hopscotch, and shinny.

The place for properly raised daughters was in the home. Girls graduated from baking mud pies to baking biscuit and cake under their mother's watchful eye. They helped with the housecleaning, the family sewing. Not that being a "home girl" meant nothing but work. In a natty bicycle costume that offered a glimpse of leggings and bloomers beneath a divided skirt, she was off on "bike picnics". In long, swishy skirts she played at tennis and golf. Despite her mother's disapproving frown, she spiced her conversation with such slang as "nit" for "no", "swagger" for "style", "grit" or "sand" for "courage", "I don't tumble to that," "You make me tired," and "It suits me down to the ground." Taking in sewing or teaching school were suitable careers for young women who had to earn their own living. The few who took up typewriting and exposed themselves in public offices got talked about.

Most families, whether the father was a doctor, lawyer, merchant, or farmer, were solidly comfortable. They didn't hear much about the sweat-shop drudges crowded together in cold, damp tenements, with little enough clothing and never enough to eat. And as for the other extreme, they only knew what they read in the newspapers about the glittering life of "High Society in the Gilded Age." The fortunes that Big

Business had been piling up so ruthlessly out of railroads, oil wells, meat packing and mining, had created a sort of American aristocracy of steel barons and coal kings. These wined and dined from crystal and gold plate. They played expensively with racing stables and racing yachts. They built themselves million-dollar mansions and furnished them with antiques brought from European palaces. Occasionally one even bought a shoddy Old World prince to be his daughter's husband.

The year 1897 resounded to the shout of "Gold! Gold found on the Alaska-Canadian border!" The rush to the Klondike began. On foot, by steamer, by dog sled, gold hunters poured into the far North.

Another cry came from the south. "Free Cuba from Spanish misrule!" April, 1898, found the United States at war with Spain. Volunteers marched aboard troop ships, singing "Goodbye, My Honey, I'm Gone", and "There'll Be a Hot Time in the Old Town Tonight." To folks back home came news of battles, of deaths from malaria. Newspaper headlines screamed, "Remember the Maine!" "Hobson at Manila!" "The Rough Riders at San Juan Hill!" and finally, "Victory!"

The Philippine Islands were bought from Spain for twenty million dollars. The Hawaiian Islands were annexed. The United States was suddenly a world power with far-flung interests.

The year 1899 climaxed an amazing one hundred years. The century had rolled in on the wheels of the stagecoach, people read by the light of candles, lived in cities without sewers. By its end there were the railroad, the steamboat, the automobile, the electric light, and civic sanitation. The four hundredth anniversary of Columbus' voyage to America had been celebrated by a great and glittering Columbian World's Fair at Chicago.

Cozy Corners in Queen Anne Cottages

Even in the small parlor a Turkish Cozy Corner may be arranged by hanging cotton prints in Oriental design over a rod set across the corner. Scatter the sofa with cushions. Snap shots on the wall, and a potted plant on a low tabouret, are pretty touches.

Magazines gave directions on how to make that newest-of-the-new—a cozy corner. Families with marriageable daughters found such a romantic retreat, where courting could be carried on in moderate privacy, a social necessity. It was a helpless parlor indeed that couldn't provide a Japanese cozy corner with a bright-flowered paper parasol sheltering a soft-cushioned sofa, or an American cozy corner with crossed flags above red-white-and-blue cushions.

A prospective home builder had a choice of various architectural styles. The quaint Queen Anne cottage was a modest one-story wooden house, painted white or gray, with steep roof, green blinds, and a narrow front porch with ornamental railing and post brackets. The Romanesque mansion of red sandstone or gray granite, or even of red or green stained shingles, stressed picturesque round arches and a huge circular porch under a conical roof. A two-story round tower opening into the parlor on the first floor made a fine dressing room for the second-story front bedroom. The World's Fair Classic style, popularized by the handsome buildings at the Columbian Exposition, revived interest in white columns in assorted sizes under a hip roof crested by a white wooden balustrade.

"Space saving" wasn't yet in the home-builder's dictionary. Goodness knows, folks needed plenty of space for all the knickknacks they collected—china figurines, hand-painted sea shells, peacock feathers standing in gilded vases. Gold-patterned wallpaper, window panels of ecru lace, and a "parlor square" on waxed hardwood floor, set a proper background for a mahogany center table, matching sofa and chairs done in tapestry plush, and a glass-enclosed curio cabinet. An electric bulb hanging on a wire lighted up the room like the sun, but a kerosene-burning silk-shaded lamp tall enough to stand on the floor was the height of fashion.

Through twinkling, clinking, beaded portieres one passed from the parlor to the dining room with its golden-oak table and chairs and marble-topped sideboard. A golden-oak bureau was in the bedroom, but the bedstead was brass or white-enameled iron.

Bathrooms were still somewhat in the nature of luxuries. Even in new houses the bathroom gave the impression of being something tacked on at the last minute, usually consisting of a narrow space partitioned off the upstairs hall or the end of the back porch. There was a white-enameled iron tub raised on claw-foot legs, a lavatory with flowers painted in the bowl, and a cast-iron toilet flushed from a high water tank with a dangling chain. Much appreciated when a lady had to strip off her "knit union suit" on a wintry Saturday night was the kerosene-burning portable heater.

> "No wood, no coal, no ashes to lug,
> Yet one cent per hour keeps you snug."

The Convenient Baking Powder

A few homes had wire screens in the windows and doors to keep out flies, but the fly fan of fringed paper on a wooden swing still hung above many dining room tables, with mamma taking an occasional pull at the cord that set the fan to swishing. The table beneath the fly brush was likely to groan under the weight of the good solid food spread upon it. Folks expected to grow fat and there was no hullaballoo of dieting fads to take the pleasure out of tasty cookery. Feminine figures that lacked a well-rounded bosom and hips were shocking problems to the dressmaker; so the female population comfortably rounded out their figures with half a dozen starches at a meal—baked beans, creamed potato, rice and gravy, macaroni with cheese, and hot buttered biscuit.

Canned goods, such as salmon, meats, and tomatoes, were viewed somewhat suspiciously, because of cases of food poisoning traced to contents of cans that had "puffed". The adventurous homemaker, however, could experiment with a number of ready-prepared foods. There was a vegetable shortening advertised as more healthful than hog lard. Gelatin powder was put up in paper packages, cocoa powder in boxes, a salad dressing in bottles. A beef extract in small cubes merely needed the addition of boiling water and salt to become a delicious bouillon. A pancake flour of wheat, corn, and rice combined was "self-rising and ready for immediate use." Because it was difficult to achieve the exact measurements of soda and cream-of-tartar for successful breads and biscuits, a canned baking powder "blended of correct proportions of soda, cream-of-tartar, and flour to preserve the mixture" met with an instant welcome.

Kitchens were huge. Nobody had started worrying about how many steps must be taken from pantry to stove to dining table. A boxed-in sink with hand pump, if there were no water faucet, was an appreciated convenience. Among the new mechanical kitchen aids, a food grinder operated by a handle proved much quicker than the old-style wooden bowl and rocking knife. The rotary egg beater was a timesaver too, but the bread dough mixer didn't fulfill expectations. A cork-insulated ice chest to stand on the back porch was fine. But grandest of all, in the estimation of the younger generation, was the multiple-motion ice cream freezer. The boy or girl who turned the crank earned the right to lick the paddle.

Quillers, Puffers, Tuckers

With mechanical aids in the kitchen and a sewing machine upstairs, husbands were sure wives wouldn't know how to pass their time, but their wives knew exactly what to do. They sat down at their sewing machines, opened up their boxes of quillers, puffers, tuckers, and rufflers, and prepared to copy "the latest Paris fashions" pictured in their magazines.

Adjustable wire dress forms, which folded up like an umbrella when not in use, and the booming paper pattern business did their part to keep feminine America informed on the latest fashions. The early eighties favored the molded effect of boned bodice, long tight sleeves, and narrow tie-back skirt. By mid-decade the bustle had returned. Supported by a cotton-stuffed pad or a basketlike arrangement of wire or whalebone, trains trailed a yard or more on the ground. Bodices remained plain, but there was nothing plain about the skirts. Assisted by the sewing machine's swift needle, fancy roamed free in kilt pleats, draped tunics, and velvet loops.

The nineties ushered in the gored skirt, smooth about the hips, billowing about the toes. Trimming moved upward to huge puffed sleeves and a ribbon wound about the neck. Now the bodice became a shirtwaist, separate and different from the skirt. Hair was worn in puffs on top of the head, and curled bangs, a product of curling irons thrust down a lamp chimney to heat, tumbled about the forehead. The mannish sailor hat shared honors with luscious creations of ribbons, flowers, and feathers. Shoes were painfully pointed of toe.

Mail order catalogues spread tempting pictures of "mohair street costumes, elegantly braided," and "velvet capes edged in fur." One could also order gauze vests, nipped-in-at-the-waist corsets, cambric corset covers, ruffled drawers, ruffled petticoats, and the new knit union suit that fitted like a second skin from instep to neck and felt so snug in cold weather.

Magazine advertisements urged men to be well dressed the easy and inexpensive way. "Instead of going to a tailor, try a Ready-Tailored Suit at half the tailor's price. $10 Suit or Overcoat made to your measure. Full Dress Suits $25. Catalogue with samples free." Fashion doomed men to plain dark suits. The knee-length Prince Albert coat demanded a silk topper for daytime formalities. Businessmen favored the short sack coat worn with a bowl-shaped derby, flat-crowned felt, or straw hat. The once admired beard was fighting a losing battle with the razor. Only the mustache remained, known, according to cut, as the strainer, the walrus, or the handle-bar.

A girl looked like a fashion plate in a tie-back skirt and tight sleeves, or in a gored skirt and puffed sleeves. A boy went to school in flannel knickerbockers and a belted blouse and to church in a "little man's outfit" of cutaway coat, long tight trousers, and a derby hat. But woe betide the small boy doomed to romantic duds—to plaid kilts (loudly despised as skirts), to lace-collared, silk-sashed black velvet suits à la Little Lord Fauntleroy. Not even the toughest freckle-faced boy was safe from his mother's fond desire to make him look like a story book princeling and brush his hair around a broomstick to make it curl.

Bicycles, Buggies, and the Lightning Route

The clang of the bicycle bell was heard in the land. Everyone was riding a bike. Lovely ladies put on knee-length skirts over full bloomers and high-laced boots and embarked on bicycle picnics, bicycle courtships, bicycle tours, and bicycle races with mustached young men in knickerbocker pants and plaid stockings. Paths for cycling were laid out alongside roads. Laws were passed forbidding cyclists to ride with hands off the handle bars. The man who owned a tandem was popular with the ladies, though, heaven knows, he paid for it. The fair sex didn't feel called upon to supply any great amount of motive power, not with a strong man perched on the seat behind and peddling for dear life.

In spite of the bicycle craze, the nation's horses were kept busy pulling people around in carriages, buggies, and phaetons. Father had to pay ninety dollars for a "Canopy-Top Surrey with rubber-tired wheels and detachable Oil Lamps," but for only $29.85 he could get a neat buggy with black oilcloth curtains to button on in case of rain.

For half a century city folks had been riding on streetcars pulled by horses. Now they could ride on the new electric trolley cars. America's first completely electrified street railway system was put into operation at Montgomery, Alabama, in 1886. Within two years trolley cars were clanking over 138 miles of track in 34 cities. Indeed, it became quite the thing to take your best girl for an outing on the "lightning route" —out to the end of the line for a nickel, reverse trolley, and a nickel to return.

Railroads were making quite a showing with the 93,000 miles of track in 1880 increased to 190,000 by 1899. For the price of a ticket one rode in a day coach on prickly red plush seats. For the price of a ticket plus Pullman fare, one sat on green velvet in a parlor car or snoozed in a sleeper's upper or lower berth.

Railroad competition was bringing the canal boat era to a close. River steamers, too, were feeling the railroad's pinch. Pushed from the turnpikes by branch line railroads, the stagecoaches trundled westward to find new usefulness in carrying passengers and mail from railroad station to remote settlements.

A hankering to see the sights of Europe caused thousands of tourists to undertake an ocean voyage. The crossing now took only about seven and one-half days. The newest liners looked quite different from the steamships of only a few years past. Masts remained, but sails were seldom hoisted. By 1890, a white-painted wooden superstructure of "decks above deck" showed above the iron hull. A traveler reported enthusiastically: "Everywhere is magnificence undreamed of. The saloons, music and smoking rooms are exceedingly elegant. The ship's band plays on deck in the evening." For other passengers the crossing was not so pleasant. Larger ships meant more space in the hold than was needed for fuel storage, space that could be filled up with cheap-rate passengers. Now began the "foul steerage" era of steamship travel when hundreds of men, women, and children were crowded below deck in a dim-lit place smelling of mice and cockroaches.

By steamship, railroad train, horse carriage, and rickshaw, a young newspaper woman calling herself Nellie Bly raced time around the world. She sailed eastward from New York in November, 1889, and arrived from the west exactly 72 days, 6 hours, and 11 minutes later.

Nellie Bly's exploit was hailed as marvelous. Less flattering opinions were hurled at the mechanics who fastened bicycle wheels to buggy bodies, installed a gasoline engine under the seat, and went putt-putting down the road, scaring the wits out of human beings and beasts.

The gasoline automobile made its American debut in 1892, but the public was wary of risking its neck and dignity in any such vehicle. By the end of the nineteenth century, however, one manufacturer could boast that he had built and sold twenty-five one-cylinder two-passenger runabouts at one thousand dollars each.

College Spirit

"Rah, rah, rah, for Alma Mater!" College yells and college songs nourished college spirit. On the athletic field heroes fought, bled, and died for the purple-and-gold or the crimson-and-white. Generous alumni dotted green campuses with magnificent buildings of gray stone Gothic, ivy-twined. They gave reference libraries and science labs for student experiments. Even college studies were taking on a livelier tone. The classics were taking a back seat to science, business administration, engineering, forestry, and dozens of other courses. And the elective system permitted students to choose subjects to suit themselves. No wonder the seeker after "snap courses" got mental indigestion.

At the various women's colleges life followed a pattern of serious classwork, daily chapel attendance, and gymnastic exercises in blue serge gym suits. Commencement featured white organdie frocks and the ritual of the "daisy chain". The Mississippi Industrial Institute and College at Columbus, Mississippi, opened the first state-supported school exclusively for the education of the female sex in 1884.

Under the public school system, schools were graded—eight years elementary and four years high school. In several states there were compulsory education laws. Country schools were still mostly one-room, one-teacher affairs, but city schools boasted big buildings with a room and teacher for each grade.

The German idea of a kindergarten or child garden where children learned through play was spreading over America. In rooms made bright with pictures and flowers, small pupils sang their "Good morning song" and marched to piano music. They sat in low chairs at low tables and teachers directed them in cutting paper into patterns and painting with crayons. More songs were sung, games were played, and, as the high point of the day, the teacher told a story.

A Book to Every Taste

The group in the parlor were discussing books. The older generation spoke of *Ben-Hur* in reverent tones. A young girl was reading *Three Vassar Girls Abroad* and planning to go to college and take a European art tour as these heroines did. The American scene also had its defenders. Her father quoted from Riley's *The Old Swimmin' Hole,* and her mother put in a word for *Ramona,* that wonderful novel of early California. Her younger brother piped up in praise of *Huckleberry Finn* and *Uncle Remus.* A small girl seated on a stool, her head buried in a book, was asked, "And what are you reading, my pet?" It was *Little Lord Fauntleroy,* of course.

Parents were dubious about putting *Tom Sawyer*—naughty Tom who played hookey from school—into the hands of their own little Willies and Johnnies. But they felt no qualms over *Ragged Dick* or any of the other Alger books whose brave, courteous heroes overcame bullies and rose to fame and fortune with the speed of a Fourth of July skyrocket.

Out of the yearly flood of new books, readers were hard put to know what to choose. "Book Corners" in magazines recommended *In Old Virginia, The Rise of Silas Lapham, Janice Meredith,* and *Mr. Dooley in the Hearts of His Countrymen.* A recipe for reading enjoyment might include Kipling's *Poems,* a dash of Richard Harding Davis' *Soldiers of Fortune,* spiced with John Kendricks Bangs's *House Boat on the Styx,* and topped with *The Prisoner of Zenda.*

Magazines were as varied as their readers' tastes: the highbrow *Atlantic,* the literary *Scribner's,* the feminine *Ladies' Home Journal. The Youth's Companion* described itself as a "national family paper". *The Chatauquan* was a cultural publication for the home circle.

Father glanced through the morning paper with his breakfast coffee; cracker-barrel loungers dozed over it at the village store. Through the newspapers folks kept up with such exciting events as the Klondike gold rush and the Corbett-Fitzsimmons prizefight. Bicycle enthusiasts read the column headed "With the Wheelmen." Young readers grabbed for the new comic picture-strips, "The Yellow Kid", and "The

Katzenjammer Kids" with small Hans and Fritz playing funny
jokes on "der Captain".

The White Killer

No home bookshelf was complete without a few medical
books. But the aid these pages offered seemed useless against
"the great white killer" known as consumption or the lung
disease. Thousands of people, many of them young boys and
girls, died each year of wasting fevers and racking coughs.
Help, however, was at hand. A German scientist, Koch, in
1882, traced the disease to the *tubercle bacillus*—so called because the germ was shaped like a tiny rod or tube. It was
proved that tuberculosis, or TB, as people now began to call
the sickness, could be cured by rest in bed, nourishing food,
and clean fresh air.

Medical science was striding forward. The dread cry of
"Mad dog!" began to lose some of its terrors after the French
scientist, Pasteur, in 1885, perfected his hydrophobia vaccine.
In Germany, in 1895, Röntgen developed the X-ray—a
miraculous machine that took pictures of the insides of men's
bodies. An antitoxin treatment for diphtheria was used successfully. Other bacilli were identified as the cause of cholera,
typhoid, tetanus, and meningitis.

But how to get rid of these horrid germs now that they
were recognized? One answer seemed to be in the purification
of drinking water, inspection of milk, inspection of garbage
disposal. Germs and cleanliness just didn't seem to go together.

The Spanish-American War, with its outbreak of camp
diseases, proved that germs were always ready for business.
In overcrowded, unsanitary camps, such sicknesses as dysentery, typhus, yellow fever, and malaria killed more American
soldiers than did the Spanish guns.

For generations people had blamed malarial fever upon

swamp miasmas. The very name *malaria* meant bad air. The terrible yellow fever epidemics had also been attributed to atmospheric conditions. Now came hints, vague but none the less startling, that possibly it was the bite of mosquitoes that spread the disease. People didn't laugh as they might have done a hundred years earlier. Medical science had come up with other queer ideas that eased human suffering, so, maybe, there was something to this malaria-mosquito theory.

Circus Day

It was a big day for everybody when the circus rolled into town on its own railroad train and switched off on a siding. Baggage cars carried the tents, the folding seats; flat cars bore the animal cages and the gay red wagons roped down under canvas. Boys popped up from nowhere to watch the unloading. Almost in the twinkling of an eye the show was massing for the grand parade. The crowd that jammed Main Street swayed back to clear the way. On came the gorgeous red-and-gold calliope drawn by six white horses, its steam-organ pipes pouring out tunes loud enough to split the eardrums. On came the camels, the zebras, the ponies with their monkey riders, the mysteriously closed red vans, the prancing white-faced, red-nosed clowns, the elephants with lovely ladies smiling and waving from little silk-hung houses on the great beasts' backs. The afternoon and evening performances under the Big Top were filled with more spangled thrills and astounding sights. Fierce lions and tigers leaped through hoops. Trapeze artists risked their necks on the high wire. Bareback riders, in gauzy skirts, balanced on one toe, and a star acrobat turned a twister over four elephants and six horses. And not to be forgotten were the side shows—the Siamese Twins, the Dog-faced Boy, and, of course, the prancing ponies and gilded chariots on the dizzily whirling merry-go-round.

Ballroom dancing passed from the stately lancers and the quadrille to the lively two-step, the run-kick-hop of the military schottische, and the backward-bending, prancing step of the cakewalk. Ladies enjoyed afternoon euchre and five-hundred parties, with hand-painted tallies, and gold-headed hatpins for prizes.

Showboats had almost vanished from the rivers, but the city theaters were producing such successes as *Trilby*, *Rip Van Winkle*, and *Ben-Hur*, the latter staging a thrilling chariot race with real horses running on a treadmill. Magic lantern slides, picturing "The Drunkard's Daughter" and "The Drunkard's Reform", were shown in lodge halls and Sunday school rooms.

Something new, and not entirely approved, were the moving pictures shown on machines set up in penny arcades. One put the eye to a peephole, turned a crank, and glimpsed a flickering half-minute movie of a performing dog or a toe dancer. By 1896, motion pictures had achieved a fifty-foot film and lasted all of four minutes. On a screen one could see the historic *Execution of Mary Queen of the Scots;* also a little item titled *The Kiss*. No one paid much attention, though, to these freakish bits of film.

Suitable Songs to Sing to the Organ

A new and cherished piece of furniture was the parlor organ with its roll-back top, carpeted pedals, and ornamental brackets to hold a pair of oil lamps. There was also a revolving stool to hold a young lady in a bustle-back frock, who had to struggle to keep fingers and feet going at the same time. It was important to remember to pull the stops—"vox humana" for high dramatic phrases, "full fifteenth" for magnificent volume when enthusiastic singers were swinging into the chorus of "Moonlight at Killarney" or "Mother Is the Best Friend after All."

To a sprightly thumping the organ gave out dance tunes for lively feet, or was equally useful on a good rolling accompaniment to Sunday afternoon hymn singing. The organ's price, $27.50 and up, was putting instrumental music into the home of the moderate-income family. The mahogany-cased grand piano, priced at $1,000 to $2,000, fitted the purse and the drawing room of the mansion owner. But the keys of both organ and piano rippled to jolly Irish melodies or sweetly sentimental love songs. Flip through the stack of new sheet music and lay aside "Hi, Ho, Let Her Go, Gallagher", "In the Evening by the Moonlight", "I'll Take You Home Again, Kathleen."

Something quite different, not music by the people but music as a social event for the carriage crowd, was grand opera. Newspapers reported opening night at the Metropolitan, October 22, 1883, as "a glittering assemblage where costumes of the audience vied with the golden-voiced performance of Faust by Signor Campanini, and Marguerite by Mme. Nilsson."

Music store windows displayed instruments in variety—flutes, fiddles, trumpets, Autoharps, and accordions. But one didn't have to be a musician to be able to make music in this advanced age. The phonograph had appeared on the scene with a music cylinder shaped like a tomato can, and a horn like a full-blown morning-glory. At first the necessity of clamping on a pair of earphones limited the enjoyment of phonograph music to two or three listeners at a time. Then the amplifying horn was added so all could hear. The same machine served for recording and reproduction. To make more than one record the musician had to perform again; or as many as seven machines could be grouped to catch the sound.

Most folks, though, liked to make their own music. Boys and girls out on a hay ride tunefully serenaded the passing public with "Ta-Ra-Ra Boom-Der-E", "Over the Garden Wall", and "My Sweetheart's the Man in the Moon". Now "O Promise Me" began its long career as the solo to be sung just before brides swept up flower-strewn aisles on Papa's arm. Now pompadoured girls in puff sleeves and five-yard skirts waltzed round and round with mustachioed gentlemen while humming the beguiling strains of "Little Annie Rooney" and "My Wild Irish Rose". They whistled while doing the cakewalk to the ragtime beat of "There'll Be a Hot Time in the Old Town Tonight." But if they belonged to the bicycle set, "Daisy Bell" was their song:

> Daisy, Daisy, give me your answer, do.
> I'm half crazy, all for the love of you.
> It won't be a stylish marriage,
> I can't afford a carriage,
> But you'll look sweet, upon the seat,
> Of a bicycle built for two.

Chapter 10

TWENTIETH-CENTURY SPEED-UP (1900-1919)

Hail to the New Century! A half million American homes lighted by electricity. One family in every thirteen the proud possessor of a telephone. Automobiles rushing along at twenty miles per hour. By 1902 two messages sent by Mr. Marconi across the Atlantic Ocean without benefit of wires. By 1903 the first airplane flight made by the Wright brothers.

HONK, HONK! Here comes the little red automobile. Already the automobile, the once-laughed-at horseless carriage, was putting America on wheels. Gentlemen in goggles and linen dusters, and ladies wearing picture hats tied on with three yards of chiffon veil, went careening down roads in automobiles without tops, without windshields, even without doors. The clanging alarm gong was not really necessary, for the one-cylinder exhaust could be heard half a mile away. And neither two-passenger runabout nor five-passenger touring car, painted white or red, could miss being seen.

Graveled roads were good enough for families taking an

174

airing in their "folding-top buggy complete with rubber tires" or maybe their "canopy-top surrey" with fringe all around. But automobile owners were raising such a clamor for roads that weren't perpetually sandy, muddy, or rutted, that presently every state had its few miles of hard-surfaced "Three-Twenty-One" highway—three years to build, twenty years to pay for, and one year to wear out.

Despite frequent bogging down in mudholes, running out of gas, and stopping every few miles because of engine trouble, tire trouble, or merely to fill the water tank, the automobile was getting about. In 1903 the first transcontinental motor trip, from San Francisco to New York, was accomplished in sixty-four days.

Young folks were hopping into automobiles and riding ten or twenty miles to a picnic or a dance or into town to see that new thing called a "moving picture". They were also enjoying another mechanical marvel, the phonograph. At informal porch parties, while some played bridge whist by the soft glow of Japanese lanterns, others would be waltzing to the lilting strains of "In the Good Old Summer Time". At swimming parties the boys showed off their fancy diving; the girls, well covered up in knee-length bathing frocks and long black stockings, just splashed around a bit. Talk was spiced with the latest slang: "Oh, babe," "Oh, you kid," "I should worry," "Skiddoo."

Magazines were beginning to exert an enormous influence both through their advertisements and their reading matter. Women hopefully tried out the make-housework-easy gadgets in the ads, even though the washers, sweepers, and bread mixers were so clumsy to operate that it took less effort to do the work by hand. Household magazines of 1900 offered suggestions on how to make "pin money from the garden" and promote "church socials." A few years later there were columns of advice to timid females venturing out into the business world: "giggling, tearful or unpunctual women are absurd in a business office." Presently there were articles on suffrage and equal rights, though certain less modern-minded publications printed horrified comments on "those hobble-skirted females who carry votes-for-women banners and march with the strikers."

Religion and social service met on the magazine pages. Bold black print asked: "How can the Church help those ill-nourished child workers in mine and factory?" "How can the Church combat the evil of the saloon and the pool hall?" Pictures showed church basements opened seven nights a week to serve ten-cent suppers to working women; showed church-sponsored kindergartens and boys' clubs that combined the Gospel with baseball.

In sober truth, something needed to be done for the nation's poor. President "Teddy" Roosevelt was strenuously trust-busting the "oil octopus", the meat-packing trusts, and any other greedy monopolies that got in the way of his "big stick". But factory workers continued to drudge long hours for low pay, and "factory town" remained a core of grim-looking brick and sheet-iron structures ringed about by shacks that were scorching hot in summer, freezing cold in winter, and where several households shared a water faucet in the yard and an outdoor toilet. The poor and underpaid of the city huddled in damp, stinking tenements that were breeding places of disease and crime. To these wretched people the hilltop mansions set amid green lawns and gardens, and the cozy bungalows and white-painted cottages that edged mile upon mile of tree-shaded streets, seemed part of another world. Strikes for higher pay and better living conditions seemed only to end in broken heads and strike-breakers taking over the jobs.

In spite of certain nation-shaking disasters—the tidal wave that rolled over Galveston, the earthquake and fire that devastated San Francisco, the boll weevil hordes that swarmed across the South and devoured millions of bales of cotton in the boll—the first fourteen years of the twentieth century were pleasant, progressive years. In 1904 everyone was humming "Meet Me in St. Louis," a musical invitation to attend the Louisiana Purchase Exposition. Three new states were added: Oklahoma in 1906, New Mexico and Arizona in 1910. Commander Peary went to the North Pole in 1909. The Panama Canal was completed in 1914, and thus shortened the sea route from New York to California by thousands of miles.

June 28, 1914: All over the country families relaxed after the day's work. Phonograph records whirled and the syncopated beat of "Too Much Mustard" was wafted on the breeze. Girls in organdie and young men in white flannels lightfootedly danced the tango, all unaware that the Austrian archduke, Franz Ferdinand, had just been murdered in a Balkan mountain town called Sarajevo—a far-away happening, but one that was to change the face of the world, America included.

War flared in Europe. Early in August Germany declared war on France. Great Britain declared war on Germany. Other nations were drawn into the struggle.

To Americans the war was something terrible but distant. A safeguarding ocean lay between. But German U-boats brought ruthless sea warfare to America's very doorsteps. On April 6, 1917, the Congress of the United States declared war on Germany.

President Woodrow Wilson's stirring call to "make the world safe for democracy" ushered America into World War. Reaching into homes, schools, businesses, the draft tapped all males between the ages of twenty-one and thirty-one for the armed services. Simultaneously America was rushing into making ammunition, guns, tanks, airplanes, and "ships for the bridge to France." In late 1917 transports were carrying fifty

1. Submarine blockade. 2. Popular Pacific 4-6-2 engine. 3. World
War I trenches.

thousand men a month to Europe. By July, 1918, soldiers were going over at the rate of ten thousand a day. Fresh from training camp, American "doughboys" were plunged into trench warfare, into the horrors of "No-Man's Land" and its mud, lice, blood, and death.

Posters shouted, "Buy Liberty Bonds!" "Save Sugar, Save Meat, Save Wheat." Soldiers and civilians stood together in camp sings and community sings, lifted voices in "There's a Long, Long Trail", in "Good-bye Broadway, Hello France", and "Over There". In homes there was a heart-breaking time of casualty lists, of censored letters from "Somewhere in France." There were war weddings, war widows, war babies. Soon the war began to move women out of work at home into man's work, to fill in for men shipped to the battle front. Women crowded into office and factory, turned farmerette. Many put on gauze masks and helped fight the flu epidemic. Others went overseas as Red Cross nurses and canteen workers. Some put on Army, Navy, and Marine Corps uniforms and were sent abroad to drive ambulances and do non-combat jobs.

The war rolled on its bloody way. Automobiles were armor-plated, had a cannon mounted on the top, and became huge, clumsy, death-dealing tanks. Airplanes soared aloft to battle the enemy. Aces of the air, their guns blazing above the clouds, made their kill or plunged earthward in flames. Foot soldiers charged up from muddy trenches. Red Cross ambulances brought in the wounded.

Then, late in 1918, the war was suddenly over. On November 11—on the eleventh hour of the eleventh day of the eleventh month, the Armistice was signed. VICTORY! America went wild. People paraded down streets, horns blowing, everybody shouting. VICTORY! The boys were coming home.

Little Red Runabout

Until World War I made "aeroplane"—soon clipped to "airplane"—a common word, the idea of folks flying around with gasoline-powered wings had been something to joke about. In December, 1903, the Wrights flew a heavier-than-air machine nearly a thousand feet along North Carolina's sandy shore. By 1909 they'd got so expert at keeping their pusher-model biplane off the ground that they flew for ten miles at a rate of forty-two miles per hour. "Marvelous," people cried, "but what is the use of it? Who wants to make journeys sitting on the edge of a lower wing, feet braced against a bar, and nothing between him and the earth but the sky?" In 1911 a daredevil pilot winged across the continent in eighty-two hours flying time. But the trip, counting time lost making repairs and waiting for flying weather, took forty-nine days. Walking would have been almost as speedy, and certainly safer. After the war, men who had flown war planes in Europe went barnstorming about America, stunted in loop-the-loops above county fairs, took passengers for a sky ride at five dollars for fifteen minutes, and got folks somewhat accustomed to seeing man-made birds. In 1918 a daily airmail was established between New York and Washington.

The "little red runabout" was chugging down the road before the plane got into the air. The automobile of 1900 looked very much like a buggy mounted on bicycle wheels. The motor was hidden beneath the driver's seat. Containers for oil, gasoline, and water were in a rear compartment. Steering was done by a tiller stick. If a folding or canopy top was desired, it had to be purchased separately. Steamers and electrics competed with the gasoline-propelled car. The electrics recommended their "noiseless and odorless phaetons and broughams" as particularly suited to lady drivers. But most automobilists were male, and they were fascinated by the power behind the gasoline engine.

Some of the horseless-carriage look disappeared when the motor was moved from under the seat and put out front under a hood. But speeds continued low, seats high, and tops were generally kept folded back, as a raised top made a car clumsy to guide. Hand cranking, pitting one's strength against a balky engine, then leaping to adjust spark and gas levers amid wild roarings, remained a wrist-cracking chore till the invention of the self-starter. Models ranged from snappy run-about to high-riding touring car with handy waterproof curtains neatly folded under the back seat, ready to be yanked out and buttoned to the side rods in case of a sudden rain-storm. Instead of curtains, costly limousines offered sliding-glass windows.

Railroaders looked down their noses at the automobile. It was a nice little toy, but not in the same class with their giant ten-wheelers hauling mile-long trains at a steady forty to fifty mile clip. The railroad was BIG BUSINESS—and knew it. Three transcontinental routes tied the Atlantic to the Pacific. Rails linked the northern lakes to the southern gulf. Bridging valleys and rivers with steel and concrete, slicing off spurs of mountains or tunneling through, rail engineers were binding America together by bands of steel. Over steel tracks the new all-steel cars rumbled—splendid sleepers with electric lights and luxurious washrooms; dining cars that were rolling restaurants; parlor cars with observation platforms.

The new all-steel luxury liners had completely lost the sailing ship look of the early steamships. Above the trim black hull rose the gleaming white superstructure topped by huge smokestacks banded in color. Advertised as "floating palaces", they had accommodations for three thousand passengers. They were speedy, too, and clipped the Atlantic crossing to six days. The big news, though, was the beginning of ship-to-ship and ship-to-shore communication by wireless or radio-telegraph. On January 23, 1909, wireless first saved lives at sea when the *Republic* was rammed by the *Florida* in a dense fog. Other ships picked up the call for help that came over the air waves, and stood by to take on passengers and crew.

World War I and German U-boats on the prowl put America's ocean grayhounds on leash. Luxury liners, stripped of their luxury and packed to overflowing with khaki-clad troops, crept across the Atlantic in convoy, their sides paint-daubed in the new art of camouflage. Across the land, steel rails hummed beneath the wheels of troop trains pounding along to the tune of "The Yanks Are Coming."

The end of the war found thousands of American families taking to the road in automobiles equipped with such wonders as cord tires on demountable rims, shock absorbers, and an electric starter that enabled women drivers to go adventuring without a strong-armed male along to do the cranking. Better cars and better roads made for increased speeds. On the few short stretches of hard-surfaced highway reckless folks hurtled along at thirty-five or even forty miles an hour.

Picture Hats on Pompadours

Feminine fashions were certainly not designed for riding in automobiles. Nothing could be less suited to a motor trip than an umbrella-sized picture hat skewered to an upswept pompadour by a jeweled hatpin an ell long. A wool pad or a mesh-wire "rat" supported the forward thrust of the pompadour.

The twentieth century opened with ladies wearing the two-piece shirtwaist-and-skirt costume—the shirtwaist made with a gracefully drooping yoke and a choker collar, the skirt gored to fit smoothly about the hips and flare about the feet. In swift succession came the stately form-fitting princess dress;

the Balkan blouse with a belt girdling the hips; the "minaret" frock with long narrow skirt and bias-flared peplum. Hobble skirts shuffled along with a hobble band tight about the knees. The "peg-top sheath" gown "immodestly" exposed as much as three inches of silken ankle. In 1915 fashion swung from hobbles to hoops—tiny hip hoops under wide skirts.

At last the younger generation could be comfortable and stylish at the same time. Little girls whose hair refused to curl could enjoy the sleek smartness of a Dutch-boy bob and a perky ribbon bow. Frocks of flounced lingerie for parties, or plaid gingham for school, were loosely belted. Big boys wore Norfolk jackets above baggy knickerbockers. Small boys were "frocked, belted, and bloomered" in Buster Brown suits. Crawlers and toddlers were joyously free in cotton "rompers".

Men were trying out new fashions too. Narrow-cut trousers changed to "peg-top"—that is, full at the hips, tight at the ankles. A few years later the first turned-up cuffs appeared on trouser legs. The short, high-buttoned sack coat was lengthened to make the "box coat" with long roll lapels. The three-piece suit of tweed or herringbone, worn with a black derby, became the businessman's uniform. A dark blue flannel coat, white flannel trousers, and a flat straw hat were favored for summer vacation time.

War put America's young men into Navy blue "sailor suits" with round white caps; into the Army's dust-colored khaki with broad-brimmed campaign hats or boat-shaped overseas caps set at a jaunty angle.

Wheatless and Meatless

The war changed America's eating habits. When the new century rolled in, housewives were spending long hours in the kitchen preparing three big meals each day. They used pounds of butter and sugar, dozens of eggs. They put three and four meats and hot breads on the table at a time, served cakes and pastries and creams for dessert.

Thanks to the U.S. Pure Food and Drug Act which became law on January 1, 1907, the American housewife could now safely serve a complete meal out of store-bought canned goods —soup, meat, fish, vegetables, with peach halves or pineapple chunks for dessert. Most homemakers kept a few cans on the pantry shelf in case of an emergency; but too frequent use of the can opener and the jiffy dessert was scorned by conscientious cooks.

In the new cookbooks the guesswork was being taken out of cookery. No more vague directions to "take what eggs you have in the house, butter the size of an apple, add what spice will sit on a knife blade." "All measurements level" was the terse command.

Up-to-the-minute kitchens boasted a white enameled iron sink, a golden-oak cabinet with "bins, drawers, pull-out shelf, and convenient storage for utensils, cereals, and spices." The golden-oak zinc-lined refrigerator was put on the back porch to keep the ice man from tracking mud on the kitchen linoleum. An oil-burning cookstove was advertised to "bake perfectly, to be clean and absolutely safe."

But World War I and the home-front slogan "Wheatless and Meatless" whisked the luscious layer cakes and rich roasts off America's dinner tables. The wheat flour, the pork, the beef must be sent to feed the soldiers. Patriotic recipes made breads out of rye, oats, and potatoes; stretched small amounts of meat by combining them with cereals in casseroles of chicken-spaghetti or hamburger-rice. Housewives saved fats by cutting out fried foods, saved fuel and labor by serving simplified meals. Anyway, there wasn't time for fixing big, fancy dinners when every hand was needed to fold Red Cross bandages. Women grabbed at kitchen labor-savers. They served fresh fruit, milk, and boxed cereal for breakfast; opened a can of meat loaf and served it with a green salad for dinner; stirred up a gelatin-powder dessert and saved hours of pie and cake baking.

Mission Furniture for the Bride's Bungalow

The newest thing in houses was the bungalow. Homemakers were entranced with its low, cozy look, its wide verandas and overhanging eaves. They were also entranced with its all-the-rooms-on-one-floor convenience, its built-in linen closets and china cupboards, its bedroom-and-bath privacy. Now, for the first time in the history of homemaking, the housewife could plan closet space to her heart's content, and make the outside of her house fit the inside.

Sweethearts sang about a "little bungalow where blue morning-glories blow"—then, as soon as the wedding trip was over, proceeded to build one of pebble-dash or green-stained shingles. The bride's mother might enjoy the elegance of a parlor complete with gas chandelier, lace window curtains, and mahogany furniture. But a bungalow had a living room with triple windows above a window seat at one end and a cobblestone fireplace flanked by bookcases at the other. Rough plastered walls made a pleasing background for bronze-finished electric light fixtures with frosted glass globes; for tan pongee curtains hand-embroidered in rust and green. The furniture, of course, was fumed oak in the popular mission style copied from hand-carpentered benches and tables found in the old Spanish missions of California. Framed of gray-brown oak, and upholstered in brown or russet-red leather, mission chairs, settees, and tables had a straight-line simplicity that was restful to eyes wearied of curves and carvings.

In a white-tiled bathroom, a white enameled iron tub stood on claw feet under a ceiling shower. The kitchen floor was covered with a pretty blue-and-white linoleum. Windows and doors all over the house were screened against germ-carrying flies.

Battling the Bugs

America was suddenly germ-conscious. Swat those flies! Boil baby's toys! Buy pasteurized milk! "Battling the bugs" became the slogan in the fight against squirmy germs and measly microbes. Modern-minded mothers no longer tied smelly bags of asafetida around little Johnny's neck in the hope of warding off sickness. Instead, they had the family doctor inoculate Johnny with the proper serum or antitoxin to safeguard him. As for the doctor, he no longer stropped his knife on his boot. Nowadays he used a sterilized instrument, sterilized bandages, even sterilized Johnny's skin with a swabbing of disinfectant to prevent any germs from slipping in.

At last, through the work and sacrifices of Dr. Walter Reed and others, it had been definitely proved that mosquitoes, not swamp miasmas, were the carriers of malaria and yellow fever. A drive was on to rid mankind of these two deadly diseases. The method was simple—kill mosquitoes, drain off stagnant water that was a breeding place for mosquitoes, screen mosquitoes out of buildings.

This was an age of medical marvels in many fields. A generation ago it had been discovered that an old-time killer known as "the dry belly-ache" was in reality a diseased appendix. Now modern surgical skill made the removal of an appendix a fairly simple operation. Surgery had come a long way from the time when a shrieking patient was roped to the operating table, when death by gangrene was the expected aftermath to opening the human body. Thanks to the perfection of anesthesia and the development of antiseptics, the old dreadful agony under the surgeon's knife was gone forever.

Gone were the stench and poisoning from a pus-oozing wound. A trip to the white-tiled, germ-free hospital operating room became an adventure into life, not death.

In 1917 when American troops were sent to the battlefields of Europe, field hospitals, medical staffs, and Red Cross nurses were sent with them. Through use of preventive medicines, fewer American soldiers died of infectious diseases than in any similar massed assembly of men in the history of the world. Based upon the discovery that the body louse ("cootie" to the doughboy) transmits typhus fever, modern delousing methods kept this disease from spreading. Vaccination prevented small-pox. Serum shots held typhoid fever to a minimum.

On the heels of the war came the flu epidemic. In army camps crowded with soldiers, in cities crowded with war workers, the death toll mounted steadily. From October, 1918, to January, 1919, half a million Americans died of influenza. In the midst of the twentieth century's electric lights, sky-scrapers, and airplanes, time seemed to be turned back to the horrible plagues of the past. Not a section of the country was left untouched. Volunteer nurses sniffed salt water as a disin-fectant, gargled with salt water, tied on a gauze mask, and risked their lives to do what they could for the flu sufferers. Doctors worked night and day. Public buildings were turned into emergency hospitals. Medical science, however, seemed helpless to halt the onrush of the epidemic. Early in 1919 the flu vanished as mysteriously as it had come, its source still unknown, a method to combat it still undiscovered.

Reading Circle

It was good medicine for a sick child's mother to sit beside the bed and read aloud from *St. Nicholas Magazine*, *Rebecca of Sunnybrook Farm*, or *The Call of the Wild*. If the invalid were under seven, the reading was probably from *Dot and*

Tot of Merryland or *The Cozy Lion.* Loyal readers demanded books in series. Beloved of girls were the "Little Colonel" stories that carried their heroine, who so resembled her head-strong Kentucky Colonel grandfather, through many volumes and adventures. Everybody read the "Wonderful Wizard of Oz" books, and the "Billy Whiskers" series about a goat that was up to fun and frolic. Boys couldn't tear themselves away from the hair-raising adventures of Tarzan, the ape man of the African jungles.

A million readers, both old and young, enjoyed *Freckles, The Harvester, The Girl of the Limberlost.* More than a million devoured *The Shepherd of the Hills, The Trail of the Lonesome Pine,* and *Pollyanna,* "the Glad Girl of the Glad Book."

Women enjoyed belonging to a reading circle. It was a backward community, indeed, that hadn't organized a reading circle in which each member bought a volume to be passed around till all had read it. Pompadoured ladies gathered annually to pore over book lists. One chose O. Henry's collection of short stories, *The Four Million;* another had difficulty deciding between *Riders of the Purple Sage,* its "every page swept by the tangy winds of the western plains," and the homespun philosophy of *Mrs. Wiggs of the Cabbage Patch;* while a third promptly picked *The Millionaire Baby.* Eyebrows lifted—a detective story was hardly proper for a reading circle.

Notable books of nonfiction were Woodrow Wilson's *History of the American People,* and a number of splendid autobiographies by such remarkable people as blind Helen Keller, immigrant Jacob Riis, and Booker T. Washington, the great Negro educator and leader who told the story of his life and work in *Up from Slavery.*

Magazines were flourishing. In 1909 it was estimated that Americans paid out sixty million dollars annually on magazine subscriptions. Readers were offered a lavish spread of short stories, serials, articles, and colored pictures.

Through the daily newspaper, folks kept up with Mrs. Carrie Nation's progress in swinging her hatchet for temperance. They read about the completion of the Panama Canal and the Pacific cable. Men and boys looked up Ty Cobb's batting score on the sports page. Women pored over the social column and Letters to the Lovelorn. Children grabbed for the "funny" page, to laugh over the antics of Foxy Grandpa, Happy Hooligan, Mutt and Jeff, and Jiggs and Maggie.

World War I books featured stories with spy ring "villains", heroes in khaki, daredevils in "flying crates". Rookie Bill's letters to *Dere Mable* made a joke of army hardships, but *Somewhere in France* and *Over the Top* brought trench warfare right into the American home.

The Public School Triumphant

> Ring out, school bells, the glad decree:
>> To all in this Land of Liberty
>> Education now, and henceforth shall be
> Universal, Compulsory and Free.

With the founding of the district schools more than a hundred years earlier, the United States had proclaimed the duty of a democratic nation to educate its citizenry. Now it was also the duty of the citizen to be educated. By 1918 there was a compulsory education law on the books of every state. From the age of six years up until fourteen, or through the eighth grade, American boys and girls must go to school.

Kindergartens or play schools were outside the public school system. Public elementary schools, whether twenty-room city school or one-room country school, were outfitted with comfortable desk seats, blackboards, and wall maps. First-graders started off printing letters and numbers while they were still reading about "the Little Red Hen" in their primers. From large flat geographies, from chunky U.S. histories filled with dates of battles and pictures of big-whiskered generals, more advanced pupils were called to stand up in class and bound the states and territories and name the presidents. Graded series of readers offered such gems as Lincoln's "Gettysburg Address", and Lanier's "Song of the Chattahoochee". An hour's recess at noon gave time for games of fox-and-hound and baseball after the lunch baskets were emptied. The long summer vacation was supplemented by a holiday at Thanksgiving and two weeks at Christmas. Valentine's Day had its own special thrill of red hearts and sweet verses drawn from the valentine box set up on the teacher's desk.

High schools were located only in towns and cities; therefore country boys and girls often had to board away from home to get high school training. Studies were grouped into five courses—modern languages, ancient classical, history-English, science, and commercial—each leading to a diploma. The commercial course was particularly popular with girls, as its typewriting, bookkeeping, and business arithmetic prepared them to get jobs as stenographers and earn their own money. Inter-school contests, whether football, basketball, or the debating society, were chiefly for the boys. But girls shone in the commencement play and the graduation exercises.

Women's colleges offered courses in the classics, science, modern languages, art, and music. Rules remained strict: unchaperoned freshmen were not allowed off the campus, dormitory lights must be out at ten o'clock.

State universities were predominantly male, though coed attendance was on the increase. Universities and colleges presented a variety of courses leading to several degrees. Journalism students produced a daily newspaper. Glee clubs and debating teams went on tour. Student government displaced harsh authoritarian discipline, and college spirit showed up in hazing freshmen, and in bonfires and snake dances to celebrate football victories. For two years World War I snatched young men out of classrooms, or put the campus into khaki through the Reserve Officers Training Corps.

Moving Picture Magic

The rollerskating craze was on. Girls in hair ribbons and boys in Norfolk jackets skated on paved sidewalks, skated up and down the hall and around the dining room table. Huge skating rinks were built where people could skate to band music and take lessons in "plain and fancy skating and the Roller-Skate Waltz."

The century opened with ballroom dancers sedately doing the waltz and the two-step. But a ragtime beat was sending feet into a faster slide-and-glide. Soon a dancing craze was pulling the nation up out of its easy chairs and out onto the polished floor. Young and old were prancing to the jerky rhythm of the Turkey Trot, dancing cheek-to-cheek in the Bunny Hug, bending and swaying in the graceful Waltz-Hesitation. Up from South America came the Tango with its sinuous step-and-turn, starting a fad for afternoon dances known as "tango teas".

Card players were going in strong for auction bridge, a keen game that traced back through bridge whist to the old colonial game of whist.

At gaudy, glittering amusement parks fun-seekers could ride the roller coaster, Shoot the Shoots, Take a Trip to the Moon, or get delightfully lost in the Mystic Mirrored Maze. Splendid three-ring circuses toured the country.

Every town boasted a theater. The best of the Broadway hits went on the road. A lucky girl with a free-spending beau put up her hair in puffs, donned a lacy shirtwaist costume, and rode downtown on the trolley with her young man to take in the show—*Peter Pan, Rip Van Winkle, Hamlet,* or *The Wizard of Oz. Floradora* and the waltz-tune romance of *The Merry Widow,* with their catchy melodies, gorgeous leading ladies, and high-kicking chorus, set the pace for glorified musical comedy.

Moving pictures in 1900 were viewed in cheap halls known as "Nickelodeons", and were chiefly travel slides or illustrated songs. The appearance of *The Great Train Robbery* in 1903, which was a thriller showing daring attacks and breakneck pursuits, transformed the moving picture into the photoplay —a movie that told a story. For these first silent movies a "spieler" stood near the screen and helped along the action with his remarks: "John and Mary board a train. A masked man glides in behind them. What will be their fate?" Presently the movie-makers were throwing printed dialogue on the screen, and folks had to read in a hurry or miss out on what was happening. Now the motion pictures had edged into the theaters (on nights when there was no regular play), and were furnishing entertainment in two hour "screen dramas" priced at twenty-five to fifty cents; exciting serials shown every week —*The Exploits of Elaine* and *The Perils of Pauline*—stood their audiences' hair on end as their heroines hurtled down cliffs and leaped from burning buildings. The sultry-eyed vamp in *The Vampire* started the "vamp" fashion among young girls. But when *The Birth of a Nation* (1915) flashed on the screen in a splendid sweep of armies pouring across mountain and plain, audiences were overwhelmed. This was seeing history written in lightning. World War I brought its own war pictures—*The Beast of Berlin, America Invaded.* Spectators shuddered at the sight of U-boats in the Mississippi River, of huge cannon booming soundlessly. Thank goodness, people said, it was just a moving picture.

The Talking Machine

The handsomely-polished mahogany box topped by a magnificently flaring metal horn might be called a phonograph, graphophone, or gramophone by its inventors, but to an entranced public it was "the talking machine". Put on a record (either disc or cylinder according to the machine), crank the handle, and settle the family right in front of the horn. How folks laughed over the lifelike growls of the bear that treed the preacher "all on a Sunday morning."

Before many years the amplifying horn had disappeared inside improved sounding-boxes, and records were available in vast variety.

Still people gathered around the home piano to sing. They sang almost every sort of thing. Geographical locations received honorable mention in "Meet Me in St. Louis", "There's a Little Street in Heaven That They Call Broadway", "Back to Baltimore", "Where the Silvery Wabash Flows", "Missouri Waltz", "Beautiful Ohio", and "My Heart's Tonight in Texas." There was also a little grass-skirt hula number titled, "They're Wearing 'Em Higher in Hawaii". Singers got funny with Irish and blackface dialects—"Has Anybody Here Seen Kelly", and "The Darktown Strutters Ball". A railroad engineer was immortalized in the ballad of "Casey Jones".

Male quartettes harmonized on "Down by the Old Mill Stream" and "Sweet Adeline". "When a Fellow's on the Level with a Girl That's on the Square" led naturally into the pulsing rhythm of "I Can't Tell Why I Love You but I Do-oo-oo."

The wild rhythm of "Alexander's Ragtime Band" set the style for the raggedest rag of them all, "Everybody's Doing It". Shoulders swaying, fingers snapping, folks began to babble "Isch Ga-Bibble" and "That Syncopated Boogie Boo". Words didn't have to make sense. The irresistible rhythm was all that mattered.

World War I upped the slogan "A Singing Army Is a Winning Army." "Tipperary" and "Pack up Your Troubles in Your Old Kit Bag and Smile, Smile, Smile" were borrowed from the English. Then Americans burst into their own war songs. Some were of tender love—"Till We Meet Again" and "Somewhere in France". Mostly, though, they were lively ones like: "Hinky-Dinky Parlay Voo", "You're in the Army Now", "K-K-Katy", and the rousing "Over There". Seasick doughboys on camouflaged troop ships dodging German U-boats could sing with feeling:

> Mister Captain, stop the ship,
>   I want to get out and walk.
> I feel so flipperty, flopperty flip
>   I never will see New York.
> Mister Captain, stop the ship,
>   I'm sick of the raging main.
> Hi, hi, call me a cab
>   To take me home again.

Chapter 11

BOOMED, BUSTED, AND BETTERED (1920-39)

Easy Money!
Gold-diggers! Rum-runners!
Yo-yos and flag-pole sitters!
Let's go places and have fun!

THIS WAS the age of whoopee. Everybody was out to have a good time. Varsity football drew its tens of thousands of spectators. Baseball and basketball filled the bleachers with screeching, clapping fans. Golf and tennis headliners pulled crowds as big as any parade of movie stars. People scrambled for ringside seats at prize fights, or stuck their heads close to a radio to hear a voice relaying the fight blow by blow. "An uppercut to the chin! His nose is bleeding! He's down—he's down—" Sports were big money, taking in a million dollars at the gate.

People were fun-crazy. They turned on the radio to get the

ball game, or a lesson in contract bridge; twirled the dial to a
saxophone sextette shrieking "Shakin' the Blues Away" and
shook their hips doing the Charleston; went to a movie to see
Mickey Mouse; tried the Tom Thumb golf course; did a new
crossword puzzle; made a yo-yo climb right up the string.

Night clubs pulled in the customers. To the brassy blare of
a jazz band, dancers jammed the tiny square of polished floor.
Hot-spot gambling—cards, dice, put-and-take, clanging slot
machines—lifted the money right out of the suckers' pockets.

Prohibition of the manufacture and sale of alcoholic liquors
had become law in 1919, was further upheld by the Volstead
Enforcement Act of 1920. Thus ended the century-long fight
of the temperance societies against Demon Rum—or so the
good folks thought. But bootleggers and rum-runners sneaked
in the liquor under the noses of prohibition agents, and people
kept right on drinking. It became "smart" to carry a forbidden pint on the hip; "smart" to slip away to a "speakeasy"
where one knocked on a locked door, was eyed through a
peek hole, and finally was permitted inside to enjoy the thrill
of buying a drink in spite of the law.

"Let's get going" became the theme of the times. Home was
just a place to start from. Hop in the car—step on the gas.
Romance moved in a hurry too. A "guy" would meet a "gal";
they'd fall in love one day, get married the next. All too often
these hasty marriages ended in "quickie" divorces.

Even among couples that stayed married there wasn't much
sitting around home together. The man of the house was intent on his golf score, on "meeting the right fellows" and
getting a "hot tip". His wife was at the beauty parlor, bridge
club, or reading a paper at her study club. The younger set,
known as "Flaming Youth", were left to kick up the devil in
their own way. The teen-age male, variously dubbed "jelly
bean" and "drugstore cowboy", affected pomaded hair,
wrinkled socks, and bell-bottom trousers. The teen-age female,

or "flapper", displayed incredibly long legs beneath her scanty
skirt, a circle of rouge on each cheek, and a dangle of bead
necklaces, slave bracelets, enameled compact, and cigarette
case. It was modern to be pert, to crash parties to which you
were not invited, to "neck" and "pet" in parked cars. The
universal greeting was "Hi, sucker." According to sex you
were a "sheik" or a "red-hot mama". You "knew your
groceries," and "went places." "It" stood for personality-plus;
and if you didn't have "it" you were a "gone goslin' ", and
you had better "fade out of the picture."

The Florida boom, with its skyrocketing land prices, made
millionaires—on paper. Men backed off from work that put
calluses on their hands; became bond salesmen, automobile
salesmen, bootleggers. The new woman was feeling her importance as she earned her own money in business office,
advertising agency, smart dress shop.

There were splendid achievements to make the heart leap
with pride. Woman's century-long battle for equal rights
with men climaxed when women, in 1920, voted for the first
time in a presidential election. Radio broadcasting—that sending of the human voice on an air wave across the continent in
a matter of seconds—made its start this same year. On May
9, 1926, Admiral Richard Byrd and Floyd Bennett flew over
the North Pole. On May 20, 1927, a lone pilot in a lone plane
took off across the Atlantic: Lindbergh's flight from New
York to Paris—3,600 miles in 33½ hours.

There were other happenings not so splendid. The nation
rocked to the hullaballoo of the Teapot Dome oil scandals.
People were amused, or horrified, over the goings-on at the
Tennessee "Monkey Trial", the court trial of a public school
teacher who had dared to include in his science course the un-
popular theory of the evolution of man from a lower form of
life. The trial was ballyhooed into a big show, and crowds
came to jeer or cheer while lawyers argued hotly whether or

1. Dirigible. 2. Babe Ruth. 3. Red Grange. 4. The dust bowl.
5. Early broadcasting.

not the ancestors of modern man had once swung by their tails from trees.

"Easy money" was everyone's slogan. The cry was: "Get rich quick. Take a flier in the stock market. If you haven't got the money just borrow it at the bank. Put a mortgage on your home, your farm, your business, but get the money. Buy radio stocks, automobile, oil, mining stocks. They're all going up— up! Buy today. Sell tomorrow. Make yourself a million bucks."

The age of whoopee came in on the blare of jazz saxophones. It went out with a crash—the stock market crash of "Black Thursday", October 24, 1929, when prices dropped and millions of shares had to be sold for a few cents on the dollar —the stock market crash of 1929.

Borrowed money was lost. Homes, farms, businesses were lost. Chilled, frightened, hungry people stared into the face of hard times. Whoopee was gone—but mouths remained to be fed.

America was suddenly willing to stop playing and go to work. But no work was to be had. Factories were shutting down. Hard-pressed businesses were letting employees go. On the outskirts of cities "depression suburbs" spawned shacks built of packing boxes and roofed with flattened tin cans— places where homeless folks could sleep when not tramping the streets hunting for a job. No one had clocks in shanty-town, but everyone knew when it was time to slouch out and shamefacedly line up for a hand-out at the Salvation Army's soup kitchen. Hunger pangs brought on wild talk. "If factories don't open up . . . If a man is denied a chance to make an honest living . . . Well, a man has a right to live. March on Washington. Make the government do something."

In July, 1932, Franklin Delano Roosevelt, Democratic party nominee for President of the United States, boldly spoke out for all to hear, "I pledge you, I pledge myself, to a new deal for the American people." On March 4, 1933, the inaugural band music had scarcely ceased echoing before President Roosevelt went into action. A "bank holiday" was declared— all banks to remain closed while plans were made to bolster sinking currency. An embargo was ordered on outbound shipments of gold; script was to be issued if necessary to supply cash for business operations. A special session of Congress was called. The "alphabet agencies" sprang into being: the CCC (Civilian Conservation Corps), the WPA (Works Projects Administration), the NRA (National Recovery Administration) with its blue eagle insignia and fair practices codes whose purpose was to raise wages, shorten hours, create more work. The first answer to unemployment was the dole—"that no one shall go hungry." Then it was up to the WPA to provide emergency jobs at living pay. Country roads were graveled, city streets paved, sewing rooms opened. Some of the unemployed were set to painting murals on post office walls, to copying historical records. The nation rolled up its sleeves and pitched in to work. The New Deal was on its way. Under a man like F.D.R., America would whip the depression.

Spring of 1935 brought a new problem. Dust storms spread deserts of dust from the Dakotas down through Oklahoma into Texas. Dust hazed the sky, gritted the eyes, spread its lifeless gray over fields and gardens. In Oklahoma particularly, despairing farm families abandoned home and land. Now was the time of the "Okies" on the road in rattling jalopies. The government finally fought down the dust storms with windbreaks of trees planted by WPA labor.

Under the spur of the New Deal, great dams—Grand Coulee, Boulder, TVA—were thrown across turbulent rivers in an experiment at harnessing the nation's water power to provide wide regions with irrigation and cheap electricity. Slum clearance projects tore down rat-infested, germ-infested tenement houses and built model apartments where low-income families could enjoy privacy, bathrooms, and electrical conveniences. Laws were passed forbidding children to work in factories. Organized labor was granted the right of collective bargaining. Provision was made for unemployment assistance, old age pensions, an enlarged public health service. And prohibition, having proved unworkable, was repealed.

Out of the hardships of the depression years came a renewed appreciation of home and family, a more settled way of life. Surveys showed that the average American man was married, belonged to a church and lodge, had his share of civic loyalty. He made his living in the traditional professions and trades as doctor, lawyer, merchant, mechanic, farmer, and also in newer work like radio, plastics, plywood, and commercial aviation. He went to his office in a dark business suit, relaxed in comfortable slacks. The average woman had leanings toward culture through study clubs, music clubs, garden clubs, welfare and civic groups. She bought her clothes ready-made, went to the beauty parlor to have her hair curled and her nails lacquered scarlet. She had a set of overstuffed furniture in her living room, an electric refrigerator in her kitchen, and an electric washing machine, electric iron and vacuum cleaner. Often she held down a job in office or store, and, through capable short cuts, managed her home too.

Swing music was enriching the language of the younger set with "jam, jive, and jitter". According to swing lingo you had "tin ears" if the boogie-woogie beat didn't "send you out of this world." To be "in the groove" was to be inspired, "corny" was to be out of date, and "screwball" and "wacky" were hardly complimentary terms.

Swing music came over the radio, as did soap opera and world events. Listeners wondered a moment about those foreign isms—German Nazism and a silly-looking little man named Hitler; Italian Fascism and a jimber-jawed leader named Mussolini. They disapproved of Mussolini for grabbing Ethiopia from the Ethiopians, and the Japs for sending their armies into China. Then they switched the dial quickly and got the baseball scores.

Through radio and newspapers the family kept up with the kidnapping of the Lindbergh baby, the daily lives of the Dionne quintuplets, the visit of King George and Queen Elizabeth in June, 1939—which was the first visit by an English king to America. The King laid a wreath on George Washington's grave. At a state dinner at the White House the Queen wore her diamond coronet, and eighty-three guests ate from the famous gold table service. This was followed by a typical American entertainment that included cowboy songs, Negro spirituals, and folk dances. The visit ended with a picnic at the Roosevelt home at Hyde Park where the President cooked "hot dogs" for his royal guests.

Making Whoopee

"Whoopee, ain't we got fun!" The flapper and the jelly bean were really whooping it up along about 1920 at a night club, knocking their knees dancing the Charleston and the Black Bottom, thrilling to a treasure hunt in wildly speeding automobiles.

Motion picture theaters were as gorgeous as palaces. *The Queen of Sheba* could be seen in cushioned luxury—ten reels of super-colossal spectacle—or *The Covered Wagon*, a Western thriller with raiding Indians and a buffalo stampede. *Mickey Mouse, The Big Parade, What Price Glory, The King of Kings,* flicked silently across the silver screen. Then came 1927 and *The Jazz Singer*, with the actors talking a little, singing a little. The "talkies" had arrived.

Sports were headlined: Championship Prize Fights; Big League Baseball; Varsity Football. Radio broadcast the Rose Bowl game in a coast-to-coast hookup. Spectators flocked to watch golf tournaments, polo matches. Aquaplaning made a hit as a daring new water sport.

Glittering toylands dazzled children with talking-walking dolls, with miniature electric railway systems complete with trains, tracks, tunnels, signals, sidings. But what family stayed at home long enough for the children to have time to play with their toys?

Suddenly the crash of 1929 changed a lot of things in America, including folks' idea of how to have fun.

Whoopee out of Style

Homemade fun brought families and neighbors closer together. The music-minded sang, strummed, tooted. There were games to ripple the muscles and prick the wits. Players mounted wheels for inexpensive bicycle polo. The indoor athlete tested his skill at darts and table tennis. The strategist played Chinese checkers, moving bright-colored marbles across a board. For shivery thrills the lights were dimmed and a crime-clue game staged: "Who Murdered Mr. Z" or "X Marks the Spot". Card-playing reached an all-time high in popularity. Contract bridge led off with fifteen million players, only to be surpassed by the hosts of gin rummy fans.

Movie-goers got their first glimpse of colored pictures in 1935, when Technicolor presented *Becky Sharp*. Crowds flocked to see *You Can't Take It with You*, *Love Finds Andy Hardy*, *Gone with the Wind*. But the pictures people went wild over were the animated cartoons such as *Three Little Pigs*, and the Disney fantasy *Snow White and the Seven Dwarfs*.

Old-fashioned square-dancing staged a comeback with girls in full skirts and men dressed up in cowboy boots and neckerchief. Next they were dancing the polka, the schottische, and "putting the little foot" in the gay *varsovienne* of great-grandmother's day. But for really lively fun there was the Big Apple. As the band beat out a red-hot tune the dancers formed a circle. "Swing right," shouted the leader. "Truck on round." They circled right in a shuffle-toddle. "Give that Charleston kick, behind and before. Susie-Q, heel and toe." Now the leader pointed at a couple, ordered, "Shine." The circle of dancers rested, each on one knee, while the chosen pair whirled to the center to cavort in the "flea hop", the "bunny jump", or whatever step came to mind. Then the circle swung back into the dance. Feet clicked on the floor at the command to "double stomp and cut that apple; kick that mule." Feet swung high. The end came with a rush to the center, hands and faces lifted, and a shout of "Praise Allah."

Play School

Big orange-yellow school buses rolled down paved roads, fetched children to classrooms, returned them home. The automobile and the good roads movement were pushing the one-room country school into limbo. The centrally located county consolidated school—eight grades elementary and four years high school—had supplanted a dozen lesser schools. The popular one-story H-shaped floor plan provided plenty of space for classrooms, library, laboratory apparatus, and an auditorium for lectures and dramatic entertainments. Shrubbery beautified the grounds not set aside for playing fields.

At long last education had become "fun". The rule of the hickory stick vanished with the nineteenth century. Dullness and drudgery were on the way out. No more hours of pondering arithmetic problems, of memorizing names of mountains and rivers. The "project" took care of all that. In numerous schools throughout the country the kindergarten idea of learning through play had moved up into the public school system and become progressive education. The pupils selected the project themselves—whether to build a toy town, lay out an airport, take an imaginary trip. If they decided on a trip, the business of planning what route to travel, and hunting up places of historic interest to visit, made geography and history come alive. Practice in arithmetic came through figuring the cost of airplane or railroad tickets. To keep a travel journal or write letters home combined grammar and writing in a delightful way. After a few weeks a new project would be picked.

Classrooms were furnished with tables and chairs; with a sand-table on which miniature villages could be built and river systems laid out. A radio "mike" was splendid for encouraging youthful broadcasters to speak out on current events. Textbooks, borrowing from the comic strips, invited the child to study through pictures and conversation. Hot lunches at the school cafeteria were provided at low cost.

Progressive high schools, at the expense of the classics, trained students to run stores, edit newspapers, operate machines.

Colleges and universities displayed acres of impressive buildings, numbered their students in the thousands. Campuses swarmed with girls. The women's gym and the home ec building loomed as large as any for purely masculine purposes. In fact, there were hardly any "purely masculine" subjects left. Coeds had invaded the physics and chemistry labs, the medical, law, and engineering schools. Courses ranged from ancient Chaldee to gear grinding and marriage relations. Social life revolved around an enormous union building which provided pingpong tables, a radio, symphony orchestra records, and a ballroom for glittering "proms" with lavish decorations and a "name band" to play for dancing. Varsity football stars drew their fans by the hundreds of thousands, and the coach often collected a bigger salary than the president.

Best Sellers

Books that offered a short cut to knowledge made the best-seller lists. At bookstores, drugstores, and newsstands one could pick up *The Outline of History*, *The Outline of Science*, *The Story of Mankind*. A growing interest in nonfiction also made best sellers of *The Epic of America*, *How to Win Friends and Influence People*, *The Giant Quiz Book*, and *Life Begins at Forty*.

Among the talked-about novels were *The Sheik*, *Gentlemen Prefer Blondes*, *This Side of Paradise*, and *Main Street*. Readers thrilled to historical romance in *Anthony Adverse*, *Mutiny on the Bounty*, *Gone with the Wind*. They suffered with the "Okies" in *Grapes of Wrath*, chuckled over *Life with Father*, puzzled over murder mystery "whodunits".

Books for young readers were gorgeous with colored pictures, brimming with rhymes and stories. There were whole sets of "Mickey Mouse" books. There was *The Story of Ferdinand*, the little bull that loved pretty flowers.

The daily newspaper offered a variety of departments—editorials, comment columns, gossip columns, straight news, society page, woman's page, children's page, sports page, financial page, question box (answers free), theater, radio, bridge hands, crossword puzzles, as well as the funnies—Andy Gump, Popeye, and Little Orphan Annie.

Magazines were divided into the "slicks" printed on glossy paper, and the "pulps" printed on rough wood-pulp paper. The pulps, taking the place of the old dime novels, appealed to readers who favored adventure. Many of the slicks catered to women readers, carried love stories and articles on child care, cookery, and home furnishings. Pages of fashion pictures showed long-legged ladies in very short skirts.

Bobbed Hair and Bare Knees

Skirts were on the up and up. The flapper brazenly bared her knees and cut off her hair. Women stopped eating starches and sweets in an effort to achieve the boyish form—flat bosom, narrow hips, slim legs—so necessary to the stylishly short, straight-cut, belted-about-the-hips dress that was made without hooks, snaps, or buttons—"So easy to get into . . . a wriggle and it slipped right down over the head." Long coats were at least as long as the dress. Tight little cloche hats shaped like upside-down bowls were pulled on over boyish bobs. Dress shops filled plate glass windows with "satin-striped step-ins" colored flesh, pink, and orchid; with "fetching little frocks" of flat crepe, georgette, and chiffon made with boat neckline and scalloped cape collar.

Sewing machines were run by electricity instead of leg power. Paper patterns gave step-by-step directions for cutting and seaming. Adjustable dress forms made for easy fitting. And yet, for the first time in the history of civilization, a generation of women grew up not trained to the needle. Many women, of course, still sewed, but not because of necessity. It was a rare wife indeed who sewed her husband a shirt now.

"Toggery shops" provided every item of male apparel ready-made. Coats fitted tightly about the hips and the waistline vanished. Trousers widened at the feet in a bell-bottom effect. In screaming plaids and stripes this became the "jelly bean suit". It was collegiate to wear a fuzzy raccoon coat. Boom times created a boom market for silk shirts violently striped in purple, pink, and green; for striped blazer coats, checked knickers, two-toned buckskin shoes. Soft collars, buttoned on or sewn to the shirt, were seen at stylish social affairs. And for evening wear, men could be comfortable in a tux instead of bothering with flapping tails.

With women taking over the knee-length dress, with men putting on knickerbockers at the slightest excuse, children could hardly be said to have a costume of their own. Unless, of course, you counted the sweater and cap outfit for the schoolboy; the middie suit (white cotton or blue serge middie blouse and pleated skirt) for schoolgirls; and cotton play overalls for the still younger set.

The depression had no visible effect on costume except to keep folks wearing the clothes they had. But when money began rolling in again and women could go dress-shopping, they found a host of new styles awaiting them. Cut-on-the-bias skirts hugged the figure to the knees, flared about the ankles.

Presently everyone was zipping up clothes with a zipper. At the beauty shop ladies acquired scarlet-lacquered fingernails and permanent waves. They put on tiny tip-tilted "Eugenie" hats, large round "halo" hats, or tied a bright-colored kerchief under the chin. Over shimmery silk hose in the popular sand shades, they buckled gay green, blue, and scarlet sandals made with open toes and spike heels.

The Vanishing Dining Room

To many a home-builder in this fast-moving automobile age a garage was more important than a dining room. Kitchens shrank to kitchenette size as "eating out" became a family habit. And the dining room that took up space and was used only a short part of each day almost disappeared from the newest house plans.

People swarmed to the cities, lived in huge multi-family apartment houses. Old-fashioned "walk-ups" were over-shadowed by elevator-serviced, ten-, fifteen-, thirty-story skyscrapers. Two- and three-room apartments included a kitchenette; a one-room apartment called for in-a-door bed, bath and dressing closet, and an electric hot plate for any home cooking. Apartment hotels supplied maid service by the hour, sent up meals on a dumb-waiter.

The automobile was helping develop suburbs in spreading circles around the cities. Home-builders dotted the landscape with small houses in a variety of designs—white-painted Cape Cod, English half-timbered, round-arched Spanish, sprawling ranch-style, and a white-columned Southern ante-bellum style copied from the movie *Gone with the Wind*. But the newest thing was the modern house with flat roof and corner windows. Impatient people who fumed and fussed at the slowness of putting up any sort of house plank by plank joyfully hailed the "prefabs". Making their choices from a half dozen designs, they wrote out a check for a factory-fabricated house with steel-framed cement-asbestos walls, composition roof, and bathroom and kitchen plumbing ready to be hooked up to the local water main and sewer. The house arrived knocked down but with each piece numbered for quick assemblage on the home lot. Three rooms, kitchen, and bath were priced as low as $4,000.

A modern house called for "modernistic" furnishings. Chairs and sofas with curving tubular steel frames were made soft with inner-spring cushions. Crystal-top coffee tables stood on chrome legs. Electric lights glowed through translucent plastic shades. An ice refrigerator was standard kitchen equipment, but there were beginning to be electric refrigerators that not only preserved foods but manufactured ice cubes for cold drinks.

Nutrition

Count your calories! Eat and drink your vitamins!—everyone was talking diet. Over-plump ladies put themselves on reducing diets to take off ugly pounds. Modern science spoke up for energy-building diets for busy folk. In the past, men had eaten to satisfy hunger and enjoy sociability. Now was added the slogan, "Eat for Health." Bones weren't straight because a child hadn't drunk his milk. Another child couldn't keep up with his schoolwork because a sugar bun was all he had had to eat for breakfast. Nutrition experts advised: "Away with the old-time heavy breakfasts of fried steak, fried potatoes, fried pies. Serve fresh fruit, cereal, bacon, eggs, milk, tea, or coffee. And be sure Junior has his glass of orange juice."

Hail vitamins! Good-by scurvy and rickets! A whole alphabet of tiny, invisible, but health-promoting vitamins had recently been discovered in certain foods. Vitamin A, found in milk, butter, eggs, green and yellow vegetables, worked for good eyesight and a strong body. Vitamin B, in liver, whole grain bread and cereals, made good red blood and helped the digestion. Vitamin C, in oranges, apples, lemons, carrots, and lots of other fruits and vegetables, cured spongy, bleeding gums. For Vitamin D, one only needed to soak up plenty of sunshine or plenty of cod liver oil to build strong bones.

Crusades for Health

People bought Easter Seals to aid the Crippled Children's Fund. They bought Christmas Seals to further the fight against TB. A heartening thought was that tuberculosis deaths had been reduced by two-thirds since 1900. In the nation-wide fight against infantile paralysis or polio, millions of dollars were contributed; thousands of workers were trained to give the baths and massages that helped to prevent the disease from crippling its victims. Through cancer clinics people were being educated to go to the doctor with those early signs that might mean cancer; to undergo treatment by radiation or surgery to remove the threat.

Mothers approved the modern theory of keeping children well, instead of believing, as in the old days, that children had to go through their sieges of measles, mumps, and whooping cough. Compulsory vaccination before entering public school was wiping out the dread epidemics of diphtheria, smallpox, typhoid fever. Other serums were helping to stave off whooping cough and scarlet fever.

Medical science had taken over home medication. Mothers no longer brewed herb medicines. Nowadays they kept their emergency medicine cabinet—usually built into the bathroom wall behind the shaving mirror—supplied from the drugstore with sanitary packages of adhesive tape, rolls of sterilized gauze, and such tried and true aids as aspirin, tincture of iodine, milk of magnesia, bicarbonate of soda, tannic acid ointment, and rubbing alcohol.

Medical research was producing amazing discoveries. Daily hypodermic shots of insulin prolonged the lives and usefulness of sufferers from diabetes. Doses of liver extract relieved the once-fatal pernicious anemia. The tannic acid treatment for burns, if given shortly after the injury, eased pain and formed a crust which kept germs out of the wound. A hypodermic shot of tetanus antitoxin given to a person who had scratched himself on a rusty nail saved him from the horrors of death from lockjaw. Real medical miracles were the sulfa drugs that checked infection. Used against pneumonia, meningitis, and erysipelas, the sulfas made these old-time killers less dangerous.

Plastic surgery came to the aid of persons who had been disfigured in automobile wrecks or other accidents. Through skillful bone grafting and skin grafting, doctors were able to repair a smashed face. They made new eyelids out of neck skin, lips from the lining of the mouth, jawbones out of ribs, noses out of pieces of leg bone. Indeed, they were sometimes able to make the patient better looking than he'd been before his automobile smashed into the tree.

Streamlined for Speed

Mass production—an auto rolling off the factory assembly line every seven minutes—plus installment buying on the so-called "easy payment plan" put ten million automobiles on the road by 1922. Five years later there were twenty-three million rattling tin lizzies, luxuriously cushioned glass-enclosed sedans, sleek low-swung sport roadsters. A better-roads movement crisscrossed the nation with paved highways. Filling stations to supply gasoline, air, water, tires, and make motor repairs, mushroomed on street corners. In answer to the cry for speed, more speed, automobile designers came out with the streamlined car, its all-steel body presenting an unbroken, flowing line from rakishly slanted windshield to rear end. Engineers straightened many winding roads so that people could go still faster. A grisly toll of highway accidents mounted—a half million people killed in a single year. Still people bought cars. By 1935 a survey reported that in America there was one automobile to every five persons, though England had only one car to every twenty-three persons, and Italy had one to every one hundred nine. And this survey didn't include the trailers, those cozy little homes-on-wheels that were outfitted with bed, kitchenette, and living room, nor the giant highway buses that went roaring across the continent in five and a half days.

In 1934 the first streamlined railroad train whizzed from California to New York in the record-breaking time of two days and nine hours. People stared at the silver-banded streak as it flashed by, its every part streamlined for speed. On the huge diesel-electric engine the headlight, whistle, and bell were recessed; the tubelike cars were designed with covered vestibules and flush window glass. Travelers rushed to buy tickets on these swift-rolling hotels—in which they could eat, sleep, read by indirect lighting, and relax in air-conditioned comfort. Tiny roomettes offered privacy with foldaway beds and individual toilet facilities. De luxe coaches provided reclining chairs for day or night napping. If one's purse didn't justify eating in the dining car with its soup-to-nuts menu, there was the "tavern car" painted with palm tree murals or with pine-paneled walls, where, at moderate prices, one could nibble sandwiches and sip coffee. Entertainment was to be found in the lounge-observation car equipped with bar, divan-seats, and a radio to broadcast news and music.

"Speed and luxury" was the demand of people taking ocean trips. Steamships strove against motorships, coal-burners were refitted as oil-burners. The Atlantic crossing was cut to five and a half days.

Daily air service, flying single-engine open-cockpit planes, was now established between several cities. Primarily these lines were mail routes, but a few passengers were carried along, strapped in among the mail sacks. Airports were laid out for take-off and landing. By 1928 commercial airlines were operating enclosed cabin planes for the accommodation of passengers—coast-to-coast in thirty hours—one-way ticket four hundred dollars. Travelers frequently suffered airsickness; but still they flew. Speed was what they craved, and planes gave it—at an average of ninety miles per hour.

These were years in which airplane history was made. In 1926 Byrd and Bennett flew to the North Pole. In 1927 Lindbergh made the first nonstop flight from the United States to Europe. In 1928 Amelia Earhart became the first woman to fly the Atlantic. In 1931 Pangborn and Herndon made the first nonstop flight across the Pacific. In 1933 Wiley Post flew solo around the world in seven days and nineteen hours. In 1938 Howard Hughes and a crew of four circled the globe in

exactly three days, nineteen hours, eight minutes, and ten
seconds.

Already a lot of Americans had become air-minded. Hundreds of planes a day shuttled in and out of big city airports.
As early as 1934 there was a daily flight linking New York
and Los Angeles—eighteen hours westbound and sixteen hours
eastbound, with dinner trays served aloft to the fourteen
passengers. By 1935 the Pan American Clipper was flying regular schedules to Latin America. Late that same year the
China Clipper opened the Pacific route from San Francisco
to Manila—five days of island-hopping via Hawaii, Midway,
Wake, Guam. In June, 1939, the Atlantic Clipper started a
two-day passenger service between North America and
Europe. Each giant four-motored ship of the air (speed two
hundred miles per hour) provided seats for sixty passengers,
with sleeping accommodations for forty of them. Seat straps
must be buckled for the first roaring flight upward; after that
travelers could wander about, chat, smoke, watch the clouds
flit by. Instead of a tray balanced on the knees, tables were
laid in the lounge and passengers sat down to dinner. If not
inclined to conversation or a social game of cards, they could
listen to the radio.

Turn on the Radio

Canned melody was pushing the home music-maker right
off the piano stool. Why bother with music lessons when
whirling phonograph records produced a Beethoven sonata,
a concert violinist, the golden voices of opera, and also the
latest jazz?

Jazz tunes were hot, jazz titles tangy—"Hot Lips", "Red
Hot Mamma", "Rhapsody in Blue". In swanky night clubs
jazz bands played for dancing, with a "torch singer" sitting on
top of the piano. Jazz records were stamped out by the mil-

lions and sent forth to be played in juke boxes and other machines. Anyone craving hot music for a knee-knocking Charleston just slapped on a jazz record.

Then radio began putting phonographs and records out of business. Excitingly new was music plucked out of the air waves. By 1925 there were three million receiving sets in as many homes, and hundreds of broadcasting stations on the air. One could click on a snappy rhythm to accompany morning setting-up exercises, twist the knob and relax to the strains of "My Blue Heaven". Over radio one got a swing orchestra or a saxophone sextette shrieking the hits—"The Jazz Me Blues", "Love Nest", "Yes Sir, That's My Baby". One also got the Prohibition Era's musical query as to "How Are You Going To Wet Your Whistle When the Whole Darn World Goes Dry?"

The depression years found the family listening to radio crooners moaning "Brother, Can You Spare a Dime?" "It's Only a Shanty in Old Shantytown", "Who's Afraid of the Big Bad Wolf?" Presently they were listening to "Jeepers Creepers", "Shuffle off to Buffalo", "Home on the Range", and "Stardust". Before they knew it they were listening to opera.

Most Americans knew little about grand opera, thought of it as something "highbrow and foreign". Now radio joined with New York's Metropolitan Opera Company to give the whole country a chance to enjoy opera's trumpet-toned tenors, booming bassos, soaring sopranos. Throughout the season, every Saturday afternoon, thousands of radios tuned in to the "Met of the Air". Office worker, laborer, housewife, thrilled to the voice of the announcer, Milton Cross, "The great gold curtain is lifting. . . ." The talking voice faded as the glorious notes of song came winging through space. One week the opera would be *Faust*, the next *Lohengrin, Carmen, Rigoletto*. The radio audience listened, spellbound, to a matchless voice singing the tender *"Caro Nome"*:

Oh, dearest name,
Oh, name beloved.
That name forevermore
Lives within my heart.

Chapter 12

A STANDS FOR ATOM (1940-60)

An atomic bomb dropped on Japan—1945
Radioactive iodine treatment for cancer—1948
First nuclear-powered submarine, the Nautilus—*1955*
First American satellite, Explorer, *put into orbit—*
Atlas, *the "talking satellite" broadcasts Christmas*
message of peace and good will—1958

IT WAS a pleasant, sunny Sunday in early winter. Families had been to church, had a good dinner. Now mother and the girls were washing the dishes; father was stretched out on the living room couch for his usual Sunday afternoon nap; one of the boys wandered over to the radio, gave the dial a twist. Instead of music an excited voice came stridently through the air waves: "America attacked by Japan! Bombs falling on Hawaii! United States battleships blasted at Pearl Harbor!"

It was Sunday, December 7, 1941.

For two years war had been raging in Europe. On September 1, 1939, Hitler's German Nazis had invaded Poland; France and Great Britain sprang to Poland's defense. In the spring of 1940 came the Nazi invasion of Norway, Denmark, Holland, Belgium, and France. Before the end of the summer Mussolini's Italy had entered the war on the side of Germany; France had fallen; the Battle of Britain was being fought in the skies; the German hordes poured into Russia.

The Japanese sneak attack on Pearl Harbor plunged America into the conflict. On December 8, America declared war on Japan. On December 11, Germany and Italy declared war on the United States; the same day, America proclaimed a state of war existed with these two countries. But America was unready for war. While the nation's young men were being rushed from homes to army camps to troopships, General MacArthur retreated before the Japanese in the Philippines. There were almost daily sinkings of American ships by German submarines.

Home folks began praying and packing boxes for their "G.I. Joes" overseas. War romances blossomed into war weddings. Young women joined the Wacs, the Waves, and the Women's Marine Corps to release men for the fighting fronts. Women and older men worked on farms to keep the nation fed, worked in munition factories, in airplane factories. The home front folded Red Cross bandages, became hospital aides, organized blood banks, saved gasoline, saved sugar, became air raid wardens. Housewives learned to think of food in terms of ration points as well as dollars. Hearts sorrowed when casualty lists came from Europe, from the far Pacific islands.

January, 1943: In Washington, representatives of twenty-six nations banded together as the United Nations, pledged their countries to fight together till victory was won.

1942 . . . 1943 . . . 1944 . . . : Britain's grim holding, Russia's and China's unlimited manpower, plus America's fighting divisions and mechanical "know-how" for producing guns, planes, tanks, ships in almost unimaginable numbers, began to turn the tide of war in favor of the Allies. Over the radio came stirring news: Doolittle's raid above Tokyo, Eisenhower's landing in North Africa, then June 6, 1944—D-Day —and the Allied armies landing on the Normandy beaches. September—Germany invaded. October, 1944—a triumphant MacArthur back in the Philippines.

May 7, 1945: Germany surrendered to the Allies.

War in Europe was ended. But the war with Japan dragged on; some people thought it might drag on for another year, two years. Guns must still be made. More soldiers must be sent to fight in the Pacific.

Then came August 6, 1945: an American plane flew over the Japanese city of Hiroshima, dropped an atomic bomb. In a matter of seconds, much of the city and thousands of its inhabitants were blasted from the land.

On August 14, 1945, Japan surrendered: not a year, not two years, but eight days had brought war in the Pacific to an end.

The war had pushed America into world leadership. The small colonies of three centuries past had suddenly become the richest, most powerful country in the world. The United Nations, organized at San Francisco in June, 1945, to represent the hopes and fears of fifty-one sovereign nations, looked to the United States for arms to protect the weak, food to feed the hungry, money to start the wheels of world trade rolling again.

Over everything, though, like a gigantic mushroom-shaped cloud, loomed the horror threat of the atomic bomb. Another war—an atomic war—and civilization would be wiped out, mankind would be wiped out or thrust back into a brutish Stone Age existence.

But Americans were too busy to do much worrying about the future of civilization. With wartime shortages at an end, everybody was clamoring for a new automobile, a new house, a new washing machine. A great wave of activity swept the nation. Airplane factories began turning out household appliances. From the chemical industry's intricate pipes and red-hot crucibles poured a flood of synthetic drugs, plastics, textiles.

Prosperity made itself visible in speed and color. Planes flashed across the sky at three hundred miles an hour. Pink—blue—yellow—green automobiles flashed down four-lane highways. Red-painted tractors, reapers, threshers, binders, rumbled over farm lands. In huge red barns electric milking machines were making dairy farming profitable in a big way. Paved roads and rural electrification from federal power projects had wiped out the difference between country and city living. Farm housewives used the same electric toasters, mixers, deep freezes, and washing machines as the "cliff-dweller" in a twenty-story apartment house. The housewife in suburbia used them, too.

More Americans were homeowners than ever before. Around a community shopping center with a glittering supermarket, self-service laundry, beauty shop, TV and radio shop, drugstore and variety store, spread out street after street of small one-story houses, each in its own yard. Often there were two cars under the carport, and a paved terrace in back with a barbecue pit and a table for outdoor eating. Suburbia was largely made up of young couples buying their houses on time (a small down payment and many years to pay), buying their rugs and television, electric refrigerator and air-conditioner on monthly installments.

Young men and girls were marrying at an earlier age than in the generation just past. A bride often kept on at her job to help pay for the electric gadgets deemed indispensable to the modern home, or to help put her new husband through college. Indeed, it was not at all unusual for both of them to keep

1. Satellites. 2. Housing boom. 3. Missile. 4. *Nautilus* under the ice cap. 5. The new flag.

on in school after marriage. Wives took time off to have a baby, then caught up with their classes while their husbands took turns at baby-sitting.

Ten million young married couples—presently ten million, twenty million babies—out of this baby boom grew a new profession, that of baby-sitter: some responsible person to look after the baby for an hour or two while the young parents took time off to go to a movie or spend an evening with friends.

Thanks to medical science people were living longer than ever before. Thanks to monthly Social Security checks from the government these elderly folks had a small regular income to help toward their living expenses. Many enjoyed companionship in Grandma and Grandpa Clubs, others sat at home and watched the world go by on television.

Teen-agers did plenty of TV watching. They did plenty of other things too—made good grades at school, played basketball and football, marched with the school band. They followed the approved social custom of "going steady" with the chosen girl-friend or boy-friend. In blue jeans and leather jacket, in skirt and sweater, they danced to the primitive beat of rock 'n' roll. And they talked their own special language. "What's buzzin', cousin?" was the greeting; "See you later, alligator," the words of parting. They bought "go juice" for the "hot-rod" when they wanted to take an automobile ride. They were "hep" if they knew. They "goofed" if they made a mistake. An attractive girl was a "chick" or a "cool kitten". An unattractive person, whether male or female, was a "drip," a "goon," or a "freep"—a cross between a creep and a freak, and he'd better "go bury himself." After the satellite launchings, anything important was "from outer space," and you "went into orbit" around it.

Juvenile delinquency made the headlines. Vandalism, theft, even murder, were traced to hard-eyed, tough-talking teen-age gangsters armed with switchblade knives. Blame was laid on careless parents, homes broken by divorce, horror comic books, on unsuitable TV and radio programs

Through newspapers, radio, and television, people were seldom out of sight and sound of national and world happenings: the "shooting war" in Korea; the "cold war" of nerves by which the new "ism"—Communism under a Russian dictatorship—strove to undermine the free way of life in the western democracies. Communist agents tried to stir up trouble among America's colored population, but American Negroes were absolutely loyal to their country. In 1954 the United States Supreme Court handed down a decision on the injustice of racial segregation—the decision that no one, because of race, creed, or color, should be barred from any public place, public conveyance, or right to work.

Over the air waves came news of the voyage of the atomic-powered submarine, *Nautilus*, under the polar ice cap. Another important piece of news concerning the Arctic North was the admission of Alaska, in 1959, as the forty-ninth state. Later that same year, Hawaii was voted in as the fiftieth.

For good or bad, life was full. Americans griped about high prices, high taxes. They thumbed their noses at the high cost of labor by plunging enthusiastically into the do-it-yourself movement. They contributed to health drives, Community Chest drives. They belonged to a church (surveys showed that sixty per cent of all Americans were members of some religious body) and they participated in its activities—joined a Bible class, worked with the youth group, served covered-dish suppers in church basements. Women got themselves into the new "sack" dress and were laughed at by their men. The "hula hoop" craze set children to wriggling their hips inside spinning plastic hoops colored red, yellow, or green.

People got excited about a variety of things. For a while it was "flying saucers" that folks with keen eyes or vivid imaginations saw dashing through the skies. More profitable was the uranium rush that started Geiger counters to clicking on mountain and plain. The government's announcement that a man-made earth-circling instrument-carrying satellite would soon be launched into outer space set tongues to clacking about space ships, space platforms, and trips to the moon. Then, horror upon horrors, Communist Russia got up a satellite first. In October, 1957, Russia launched its Sputnik I, followed a month later by its Sputnik II carrying aloft a small dog. Americans fell to working furiously, and in January, 1958, launched a satellite of their own, Explorer I. Then, in mid-December, 1958, the "talking satellite", Atlas, was put into orbit. From outer space sounded the voice of the President of the United States broadcasting a Christmas message to all the world: "I convey to you and to all mankind America's wish for peace on earth and good will toward men everywhere."

Marvel followed upon marvel. In March, 1959, Pioneer IV was put into orbit around the sun.

S for Shorts, Slacks, and Synthetics

> Take two cups coal tar and six cups oil,
> Flavor with salt and bring to a boil.
> Add a dash of carbolic; with soybeans sprinkle.
> Set off to cool. Iron out every wrinkle.
> Cut by pattern into skirt and waist.
> Apply trimming to individual taste.

The chemist didn't write his "Recipe for a Lady's Dress" in exactly the above words, but for better or worse the chemist was in the fashion business. More and more a lady's clothes weren't quite what they seemed. Sheer stockings started out as a lump of coal. A warm "woolen" jacket was originally skim milk. Glittering evening gowns were woven from spun glass.

The square-shouldered look was à la mode. Smart cocktail

suits, street and house dresses, sudsable seersucker play-suits and glamorous dance frocks were designed with padded shoulders, slim hips, short skirts.

The square-shouldered look showed up in men's wear, too. In particular it showed up in the "zoot suit" so admired by dance-hall hep cats. Made of flashy plaids and stripes, the zoot suit featured an extremely long coat with padded shoulders and huge lapels, high-waisted pants that ballooned at the knees, then tapered to tight ankle cuffs. This was worn with a broad-brimmed hat, string tie, and thirty-six inches of dangling watch chain.

America's entry into the war put young men, and also a number of young women, into uniform. Cloth and leather, along with a lot of other things, went to war. Government Order L-85 set yardage limitations on civilian clothing. Cuffs must be left off the bottoms of men's trousers. No more vests. Shirttails were cut so short they would hardly stay put. Women squeezed themselves into thriftily-cut frocks. Leather footwear was rationed (the only apparel so restricted) and purchase of a pair of shoes meant parting with one of the three ration stamps allowed each year. Thin cloth for babies' dresses disappeared from store shelves; so did safety pins. The rubber shortage created a crisis in infant's wear: no more rubber panties for babies—whatever their misdeeds. With silk hose almost unobtainable except in the black market, ladies were advised to buy their "stockings" at the cosmetic counter. "Stop by our Leg Bar and get a pair of hose painted on in fifteen minutes. Price $1." The fashionable shades were dusky beige and sun tan. To the chant of "It's silly to be chilly," some folks got themselves into old-time knit union suits when the fuel shortage turned their homes into iceboxes.

The lifting of restrictions at the end of the war returned cuffs to men's trousers. The vest did not return, and the resultant two-piece suit became known as the "American lounge suit". Men relaxed in bright-colored slacks, open-at-the-throat shirts, and plaid jackets; only the bravest souls appeared in public in above-the-knees Bermuda shorts. Hair was clipped in the "crew cut", the "feather crew", the "flat top".

The year 1947 introduced the New Look in feminine fashions and caused an upheaval the length and breadth of America. This new silhouette displayed delicately rounded shoulders, nipped-in waist, shapely bosom, and longer skirts. Ladies peered into mirrors and shuddered at their Old Look—shoulders padded to prizefighter proportions, skirts too short to hide knock knees. Garment manufacturers drooled in happy anticipation of rising sales. Husbands and fathers clutching their wallets howled, "Hold that hemline."

But hemlines continued to drop. Skirts were widened with crinoline petticoats, plastic hoops, a cinch to make the waist small. In contrast, the daring halter worn with shorts, slacks, pedalpusher, or skintight blue jeans showed up on the street as well as the tennis court. A fine-furred mink coat was tops in luxury. Hats shaped like upside-down flowerpots rested on hair-dos ranging from curly-top poodle-cut to dangling pony-tail. Toenails, painted scarlet to match fingernails, gleamed through sheer stretch-nylon hose. Feet tripped gaily on spike heels and foam-rubber soles, in flat ballerina slippers, in bright-colored open-toe "wedgies".

Presently waistlines dropped and the "long torso dress" was all the style. Then it was the "sack" or the "chemise" dress that bypassed the waist, tightened about the knees, bulged out in the back.

To young America clothes apparently meant dressing up like a favorite TV or funny-paper character. The Hopalong Cassidy influence put millions of boys and girls into cowboy (or cowgirl) suits. The Davy Crockett craze outfitted city dwellers in coonskin caps. Ardent space men thrust their heads inside plastic space helmets. Ordinary garb for small boys was the slack suit, Eton suit, corduroy or seersucker overalls. Tiny girls displayed ruffled can-can panties under sheer frocks. For teen-agers it was "mix-match" jackets, skirts, or trousers. For the very youngest there was the pinless diaper (it tied on), and a new stretchy creeper suit that grew with the wearer.

From the chemist's laboratory came more wonder fabrics in sunfast, tubfast colors—"easy to sew—easy to keep fresh-looking: just slosh in the wash bowl and hang up to drip-dry —no ironing—no shrinking."

Building Boom

War called a halt on home-building, put priorities on lumber, steel, cement. War almost stopped the buying of electrical conveniences. Factories that had made washing machines and vacuum cleaners were now war-geared to making airplane parts. Wartime housing shortages had cities bursting at the seams. Families snatched at any sort of shelter—auto trailer, metal Quonset hut, plywood prefabs for which the purchaser supplied foundation, roofing, electric wiring, plumbing, and labor.

The end of the war found America frantic for houses. The moment materials were released from military uses, the building boom started. Home-hungry families drew on their war-bond savings. A veteran, through government loans, could buy a house with no down payment and twenty-five years in which to pay it out at so-much-per-month. But alas, the price of houses had gone up. The pre-war five-rooms-and-bath house priced at $5,000 was now $10,000 or $15,000.

The old-time carpenter would have stared at the new assembly-line building techniques and the new materials. Solid concrete slabs were poured for foundations. Exterior walls were of cement blocks, asbestos shingles, glass brick, and plate glass. Interior storage-walls with built-in closets, shelves, and drawers were trucked in from a factory. Metal window frames came ready to set into the walls, metal cabinets ready to set up in the kitchen. Floors were laid with rubber or asphalt tile. Bright-colored plastic tops covered kitchen tables and counters. Air-conditioning made for winter warmth and summer coolness.

Favored designs were the rambling ranch style and the glass-walled modern. Specifications called for a picture window, one-and-a-half baths, and a two-car carport. People talked of "family living" in a servantless house. Floor plans showed a family room where a boiling pot, small children, and TV could be watched simultaneously.

Furniture was smooth-surfaced and lightweight. Units of chests, shelves, and tables could be grouped to individual taste to make bookcases, desks, dressing tables. Many pieces were bought unfinished and painted by do-it-yourself fans. Chairs appeared in amazing shapes and materials. The cocktail or TV chair was softly upholstered. The molded chair was shaped of foam rubber sprayed with colored plastic and supported on tubular chrome-plated legs. The sling chair was merely a length of canvas slung between bent steel rods. On a bed without headboard or footboard one slept on an airy foam-rubber mattress and kept warm under an electric blanket.

A mechanical marvel was the all-electric kitchen with range, refrigerator, dishwasher, deepfreeze, and also a laundry corner with twin washer and dryer. Instead of laboriously polishing silver knives and forks, the up-to-the-minute housewife used well-designed stainless steel flatware that never needed polishing. She cooked and served in fireproof glass, spread her table with a plastic "cloth", and ate from unbreakable plastic dishes of rainbow colors.

Heat It and Eat It

World War II had introduced America, the land of plenty, to food rationing. While the beef, bacon, and butter went to feed their fighting men, housewives learned to stretch a bit of meat with cereal, to bake Victory Cakes mixed with honey instead of sugar. And they learned to use the ration books that made it possible for scarce foods to be divided equally among all and not grabbed by a greedy few. Ration Book One had numbered stamps—stamp 25 let you buy a pound of coffee, stamp 12 was good for five pounds of sugar. In succession came books Two, Three, and Four, with their pages of colored stamps. Blue stamps were for canned fruits and vegetables, red stamps for meat, cheese, fats. The ration book stayed in the buyer's handbag with her billfold. The end of the war brought the end of rationing. It was fun to be able to go grocery-shopping again and buy steaks and roasts and sweets without having to count ration points.

Food packers now began taking the "cook" out of home cookery with a wide variety of ready-to-serve foods. Supermarkets offered such items as "minute steaks", "instant coffee", "brown-and-serve pies". A frozen foods counter yielded packages of pre-cooked meats, fish, vegetables. There were packages of rolls, biscuits, corn muffins, even frozen waffles that needed only to be crisped in the electric toaster (modern shades of great-grandma and her long-handled waffle iron at the kitchen hearth). Packages called "TV dinners" contained whole dinners, each frozen in its own aluminum-foil tray— beef-and-vegetable, turkey-and-rice, that only needed to be heated and eaten, and dishwashing saved by throwing away the tray. Enclosed in a box of cake mix was an aluminum-foil pan in which to bake the cake, and a plastic bag containing chocolate or vanilla frosting ready to spread on top.

Medical Miracles

The wonders produced by medical scientists were almost too miraculous to be true. Borrowing from the living or the dead, transplants were made of bones, skin, nerves, tendons, even of a healthy kidney to take the place of a diseased one. The grafting of a healthy cornea upon a blind eye brought the gift of sight. Powerful "atomic medicines" aided in the fight against cancer. Shots of penicillin checked infection.

One of the great medical advances that came out of the horrors of war was the "blood bank". A blood transfusion in time of illness or accident often cheated death of its victim. Many healthy persons gave or sold blood to the blood bank to be used within a few weeks as whole blood, or made into plasma. This is that part of the blood which remains after the white and red cells have been removed, and may be safely kept for several years. This blood was processed and stored at freezing temperature, ready to be used, for instance, after a traffic accident when a man lay crushed and bleeding, his face gray with the pallor that meant approaching death. A jar of blood was warmed and dripped into his veins. Within a few minutes his color began to come back; he had a chance to live.

The spring of 1955 was a landmark in the fight against polio. Hypodermic needles flashed as millions of children were given the Salk polio vaccine shots. At last there was hope of blocking off polio before it struck. To the world, America held out its gift with open hands, a gift made possible through the more than three hundred million dollars Americans had contributed through the yearly March of Dimes.

People ate a salt-free diet if they had high blood pressure. They took "shots" to relieve allergies. If they got all tied up in emotional knots they went to the psychiatrist to be psychoanalyzed. Home medication, except for the take-an-aspirin, give-it-a-swab-of-iodine sort, was no more. Even the old-fashioned family physician, as medical knowledge grew vast and complicated, was often supplanted by the specialist. People went to the hospital for check-ups and treatments as well as for surgery.

Thanks to medical science fewer babies were dying during that risky first month of life. Also, more grown-ups were living to reach the Biblical three-score-and-ten years. Geriatrics —the study of old age and its ailments—became an important branch of medicine when the U.S. population of "oldsters" (sixty-five years and over) reached the ten million mark and kept on growing.

All of us can thank the marvels of modern medical science for their effect on every American's life expectancy. A child born in the early colonial days could reasonably look forward to reaching the age of twenty-one years. In the centuries between the first settlement and 1880 that expectancy had only lengthened to thirty-four years. In the three-quarters of a century since then the life span has more than doubled—has lengthened to 69.8 years, to be exact. Again thanks to medical science, these added years can be healthy, happy, busy ones.

G.I. Joe Goes to College

The public schools were going their merry way despite occasional outcries from parents that modern schooling was "too much play and not enough book learning." Activity programs emphasized the "social-centered ideal" of how to adjust to the group. Textbooks were furnished free. A school newspaper, school band, and a system of student government gave practical application to literary, musical, and political stirrings in the youthful mind. In contrast to such dull subjects as spelling and arithmetic were courses in costume design, folk dancing, and automobile driving.

War turned colleges and universities into military training centers. The traditional four-year program that allowed time for sports, entertainments, and vacations was war-geared to three years. The need to know what foreign friend or foe was talking about increased interest in foreign languages. Not only French, German, and Russian, but also Hindustani, Afrikaans, Japanese, and a score of others were reproduced from a phonograph recording for the student. War inspired such new courses as aerodynamics and chemical warfare. At the end of the war the government set aside money to pay for the education of young men whose college career had been interrupted by their period of service in the armed forces. In 1947, more than two million veterans applied for a college education under the G.I. Bill. This influx of older students, many of them married, brought a change in campus social life. Varsity football continued to draw its crowds, but there were fewer glittering "proms", more concerts and lectures. In tune with the times, the degrees most sought after were in mechanical, electrical, and petroleum engineering, in chemistry, physics, and electronics.

The wartime baby boom was now pushing millions of pupils up to school age each year. Suddenly there was a shortage of teachers, of classrooms in which to teach.

In May, 1954, the United States Supreme Court ruled against the segregation of the white and colored races in the public schools. In many schools integration was accepted quietly and made to work. Some Southern states, however, in defiance of the court order, threatened to close their public schools rather than have them "mixed", and made plans to set up dummy organizations to run them as private institutions.

In spite of upheavals and shortages, education moved forward. New schoolhouses were built. New teaching methods were tried out. Movies came to the classroom in informative ten-minute films on such subjects as "How Bees Make

Honey", "The Growth of Cities", "Atomic Energy". Before long TV was broadcasting lessons in math, science, history, and other subjects. Over TV one teacher was able to reach students in dozens of classrooms instead of just one small group.

Many men and women, recently or long since out of school, realized their need for new skills and new knowledge in a rapidly changing world. The adult education program was the answer to their problem with its courses in economics or airplane mechanics, in business administration, foreign languages, or zoology. Through university extension courses, by radio and TV, or by enrolling in evening classes at the public schools, Americans by the thousands embarked upon part-time study projects designed to make them more useful citizens.

Book Clubs

Whether a reader's age was eight or eighty, there was a book club eager to provide suitable books. Nearly a hundred book clubs were supplying millions of readers with varied literary fare at moderate cost. Each month club members received their choice of books ranging from serious novels to mystery yarns; books on religion, history, science, sports, and music; books on how to build a better mousetrap or be a better man.

People read the daily newspaper to keep up with politics, the weather, the latest social and scientific doings. They bought oversized picture magazines, digest magazines for that spare moment's reading, weekly news magazines to keep them up to date on who's who and what's what. Giving the magazines a run for their money were the pocket-size paperback books that sold for twenty-five or more cents. During the war millions of these small books were shipped overseas to book-hungry soldiers and sailors.

War brought a demand for accounts of diplomatic intrigue and eyewitness reports from the battlefront. Grimly informative were *Berlin Diary, Here Is Your War, They Were Expendable.*

Fiction fans raced through cloak-and-dagger historicals— *The Black Rose;* religious historicals—*The Big Fisherman;* and brutally realistic war novels—*The Naked and the Dead, From Here to Eternity.* But the big news was nonfiction. Here was subject matter to every taste—the humorous family chronicle, *Cheaper by the Dozen;* humorous picture books, *The Baby* and *White Collar Zoo;* comment and personal philosophy, *Inside U.S.A.* and *Gift from the Sea.* Readers shivered at the destructive blast of the atom bomb in *Hiroshima* and *One World or None,* peered anxiously into the future in *Across the Space Frontier.* For hope and reassurance they turned to *The Power of Positive Thinking* and *How to Stop Worrying and Start Living.* Topping all best-seller lists was the *Revised Standard Version of the Bible.*

For young readers a horde of comic books copied the funny-page's method of telling a story through pictures and bits of conversation issuing visibly from the characters' mouths. "Animated" picture books squeaked, squealed, and shook. On library shelves "fact" books about rocks, oceans, weather, and electronics hobnobbed with stories of foreign lands and ancient times. Animal stories sat beside airplane adventures. But one way to ease Junior from his seat before a TV set was to hand him *The Complete Book of Space Travel.*

Jet Propelled

Americans found their pleasant habit of gadding about abruptly halted by World War II. Luxury liners were turned into troop ships. Airplane pilots went into the Ferry Command to fly bombers to England. The railroads were busy moving a million fighting men a month. Even the automobile, the civilian's own private way of travel, was ordered geared to war. Gas ration coupons permitted the purchase of a limited number of gallons of gasoline per car. "Car pools" were formed so that factory workers, businessmen, school children, could ride together and save rubber, to keep a mechanized army on its rubber-tired wheels, save gasoline to keep for the war effort.

Peace again sounded the call to the open road, the sea paths, the skyways. Railroad passengers enjoyed the thrill of riding "upstairs" in the new dome cars: from the main floor of the coach, lounge car, or sleeping car, a short stairway led up to seats under a dome of heat-and-glare-resistant glass that gave an unobstructed view of passing scenery. Diesel engines hauled all-metal streamlined cars to every corner of the nation. Dining cars provided vibrationless tables, cushioned chairs, sweet music to eat by. Sociable folk met in the club car to while away time playing games and listening to the radio.

Automobiles by the millions swarmed through city streets and country roads. As cars got longer and wider and cost more money, they were challenged by inexpensive "midget autos" imported from abroad. But all had a low, road-hugging look, and many were finished in two colors, such as blue and white, gray and scarlet. Women drivers especially approved the fingertip steering, foam-rubber cushions, automatic gear shift, power brakes, summer-winter air-conditioning, and panoramic windshield of tinted safety glass. Smooth-surfaced super-highways invited to cross-country trips. Roadside motels provided overnight accommodations for both motorist and motorcar.

Those in a hurry rode the skyways. Giant four-motor double-deck airliners, flying 340 miles per hour at 25,000 feet up, whisked passengers from New York to Hawaii in 23½ hours; from New York to London in 11 hours. Travelers

stepped on a plane in America, ate dinner, saw a movie, slept—
and awoke in England. They took round-the-world trips at
tourist rates (less than six cents a mile) and only four days'
flying time, but with leisurely stopovers for sightseeing.

The latest marvel in speedy flight was the jet liner. From
the military jet that laced the sky with wispy vapor ribbons
and was gone from sight before the roar of its engines could
be heard by watchers on the ground, sprang the jet airliner.
Flying time was cut still further. In October, 1958, daily jet
service across the Atlantic began—New York to Paris in seven
and a half hours, Los Angeles to New York in four and a
half hours. Breakfast could be eaten in California, lunch in
New York, and one could be back in California in time for
dinner—all in less than twelve hours.

Everybody Watches TV

America was full of marvels, not the least of which was
television. Above millions of rooftops, TV aerials sprouted
in a fantastic metal forest. Within millions of living rooms
viewers expectantly faced a squarish box with a glass screen.
With a twist of the dial on the box, the whole world of news,
sports, music, and entertainment was there to be both heard
and seen. Hour after hour families sat in semi-darkness, eyes
glued to figures flashing across the glowing screen. They
chuckled at the comedian's wisecracks, swayed to jazz
rhythms, tensed to the excitement of the quizzes and the give-
away shows. Viewers enthusiastically followed certain daily
or weekly programs: children rushed in from play to watch
"Howdy Doody" and "Space Patrol"; men tuned in the sports;
women preferred "I Love Lucy" and sweet music. The great
TV boom came around 1947; but the first commercial broadcast was on July 1, 1941. It lasted one minute, showed a clock
face, and a voice told the time.

Young folks were dancing the fox-trot, the rumba, and the jitterbug. Under the spell of a "hot" trumpet jitterbugging couples invented fantastic new steps. Up from Latin America came the mambo to set double-jointed teenagers to wiggling their shoulders and shaking their feet, to doing a jitterbug boogie to a Latin beat. Before long they were stomping hard and kicking high in the rock 'n' roll.

Canasta was also brought from Latin America around 1949 and tried to push gin rummy, poker, and contract bridge from the card table.

The movies were experimenting with the new "wide screen", "Todd A-O", and the still newer "3-d" pictures that had the audience shrieking and ducking in their seats to avoid the three-dimensional realism of onrushing cars and boats that seemed about to spring right out of the screen. The drive-in theaters, where people sat in their own automobiles and watched the picture on a huge screen, drew nightly crowds. Sound was brought to each car by portable microphones. Rival drive-ins competed for family patronage with such added attractions as children's playgrounds, soft drink and sandwich stands, and often a washateria: "Just let the family laundry wash itself while the family relaxes over a double feature."

No need for anyone to be bored or lonely. At the city recreation department there was fun for everybody. A lot of the fun was free. Or you could pay a dollar for membership in some special group and be doing-something-with-somebody all day and far into the night—taking up canasta, rock 'n' roll, dramatics, golf; playing a fiddle or a drum in the civic orchestra, singing in the chorus. There were playgrounds with swimming pools and baseball diamonds for the youngsters; for older people there were clubs, too. Family night brought out every age to mix happily in games and stunts, in square dances with the caller telling you just when to "salute partners", "do-si-do", and "swing corners". Above the piano's rhythmic thump sounded the call to "all join hands and circle round":

"Lift your feet and let them fall,
Swing your partner and promenade the hall."

Hi-Fi

G.I. Joe of World War II was not a singing soldier—radio did his singing for him. Along with "The Star-Spangled Banner", the radio broadcast the latest war-inspired song hits. Over the air waves came "I'm Dreaming of a White Christmas" and "When the Lights Go on Again". Invisible vocalists patriotically urged all Americans to "Praise the Lord and Pass the Ammunition", grimly warned, "You're a Sap, Mr. Jap", and called out cheerfully, "Goodbye, Mamma, I'm off to Yokohama." "Rosie the Riveter" paid honor to women working in war plants, and "My Ration Book" to belt tightening on the home front.

About this time a new word, "hi-fi", was added to the American language. In reality it was just a shortening of "high fidelity", as applied to the mechanical processes of reproducing music in the rich tones which issued from the singer's throat or violinist's bow. For years the blare of the radio had drowned out the scratch of the phonograph needle—and the old-time needles *were* scratchy. Now the new LP (long-playing) records and the clear sweetness of hi-fi tone reproduction set the grooved disks to whirling again. Hi-fi fans bought record players with diamond-point needles and powerful amplifiers. They bought at least three speakers. A big corner cabinet held the deep-voiced "woofer". Across the room a tiny "tweeter" gave forth bell-like tones in the upper register. A "squawker" filled in the middle notes. Hi-fi fans collected records: according to taste, they bought albums of opera, "sizzling platters" of jazz, symphonic masterpieces played by hundred-instrument orchestras.

Hi-fi and radio combined in the "disk jockey" who sent hours of hillbilly, cowboy, and "pop" tunes out over the airways. Listeners mooned over "The Tennessee Waltz" and "I'm Falling in Love with Love." Shoulders swayed to the rock 'n' roll rhythm of "He's a Real Gone Guy" and "Jailhouse Rock". Tongues twisted to follow the nonsense jargon of "The Purple People Eater" and "Hoopa Hoola". Minds got twisted trying to keep up with all the verses in the "Ballad of Davy Crockett".

From the founding of their nation to the present, Americans have enjoyed lifting their voices in song. Indeed, the titles of the songs they sang help tell the story of what was happening in America through the years. Beginning with such timely items as "Two on a Satellite" and "Going into Orbit around You" (1958), move backward to World War II and listen to people urging each other to "Put the Axe to the Axis" (1942). Before that, during the hard-time years of the depression, when they lived in a "Shanty in Old Shantytown" (1932), they begged, "Brother, Can You Spare a Dime?" (1932). But in the boom times before the crash that started the depression, the song was "Ain't We Got Fun" (1921). Before that, the soldiers of World War I were telling the enemy in blood-tingling tunes that they were saying "Good-bye, Broadway, Hello, France" (1918), and that they would soon be "Over There" (1917).

Americans celebrated the invention of the incandescent light bulb, the telegraph, and the telephone in "The New Electric Light" (188–), "I Guess I'll Have to Telegraph My Baby" (1898), and "Hello, Central, Give Me Heaven" (1901). And they were supremely confident that even if they felt "All In, Down and Out" (1906) you "Can't Keep a Good Man Down" (1900).

They sang about studying "readin', 'ritin' and 'rithmetic" in "Schooldays" (1907); about going to the circus—"The Animal Fair" (1870); about baseball—"Take Me Out to the Ball Game" (1908); about the sights to be seen on the exposition midway in "Meet Me in St. Louis, Louie, Meet Me at the Fair" (1904). There were songs telling about the fun they had dancing "The Cakewalk in the Sky" (1899), "Learning McFadden to Waltz" (1890), and "Tango Is the Dance for Me" (1912).

They were fascinated by the variety of ways in which they traveled about. Nearly a hundred years before they said "Thanks for the Buggy Ride" (1928), they had sung "Wait for the Wagon" (1850). The era of the steam locomotive received its due in "Riding on a Railroad Train" (1863) and "When That Midnight Choo-Choo Leaves for Alabam" (1913). The automobilist was jeeringly told to "Get Out and Get Under" (1913). But the bird-man who went "Up in a Balloon" (1869) was later issuing a cordial invitation to "Come Take a Trip in my Air-ship" (1904).

They sang of "Home, Sweet Home" (1823). "My Old Kentucky Home" (1853), "Little Gray Home in the West" (1911). They drank out of "The Old Oaken Bucket" (1817), and told their friends, "There's Always a Seat in the Parlor for You" (1881). The brave fireman won praise as "The Man with the Ladder and the Hose" (1904). And "The New England Factory Girl" (1848) was assured that "Heaven Will Protect the Working Girl" (1909).

The soldiers of the Spanish-American War sailed away singing "There'll Be a Hot Time in the Old Town Tonight" (1896). The wearers of the gray and the blue marched off to the martial strains of "Dixie" (1860) and "We Are Coming, Father Abraham" (1863). In the War of 1812 men marched and fought to "Hail Columbia" (1798). For the homespun-clad, sharpshooting soldiers of the American Revolution the tune was "Yankee-Doodle".

Pride in country was not necessarily expressed in warlike music. Peace had its songs too—"America the Beautiful", "God Bless America", and "America". The tune of this last was borrowed from the British national anthem, but the words are America's own, written in 1832 by the Rev. Samuel F. Smith. Wherever Americans gather to sing the songs they love, a moment of solemnity touches every heart as voices unite in singing:

> My country, 'tis of thee,
> Sweet land of liberty,
>   Of thee I sing:
> Land where my fathers died,
> Land of the pilgrim's pride,
> From every mountain side,
>   Let freedom ring.